Dear Reader,

You and I both hope this book lives up to its promise, nudging you to happiness. Maybe you'll consider helping to test its effectiveness, then? It's totally voluntary of course, but I'd greatly appreciate you answering a short ten-question online survey immediately before and after you use the book for 30 days.

The survey will take the temperature of your emotional health and it's based on a test often used by health professionals, so we'll discover whether you experience a difference while using the book.

You'll find the test online at:

moodnudges.com/startbook

Thanks for thinking about helping.

Jon Cousins

Nudge Your Way to Happiness

Nudge Your Way to Happiness

The 30 Day Workbook for a Happier You

JON COUSINS

Z

ZOODORA BOOKS

Zoodora Books
P.O. Box 20158
Stanford
California 94309
U.S.A.

www.zoodora.com
nudgeyourway@zoodora.com

Ordering Information:
Quantity sales. Special discounts are available on quantity purchases by corporations, associations, and others. For details, contact the publisher at the address above.

Although you can do lots to increase your own happiness, there could be times when you feel really "stuck". Now and then, unhelpful ways of thinking and negative emotions can seem overwhelming. If this happens to you and it begins to interfere with your life and your relationships, it may pay to find expert support. Asking for help is a sign of strength, rather than weakness.

ISBN 978-1-53004-260-9

First Edition
10 9 8 7 6 5 4 3 2 1

This book is dedicated to the many thousands of Moodscope and Moodnudges blog readers who gently put me right when I got it wrong, and generously patted me on the back when I occasionally got it right.

The best way out is always through.
— ROBERT FROST

Contents

Introduction

Of course you might have picked up this book out of casual interest, but it seems more likely to me that you've done so because your mood is low. Perhaps help seems hard to find?

In *Nudge Your Way to Happiness* I'll show you how you can take immediate small steps that are custom-designed to boost your mood. You'll monitor your progress as you go, so you'll actually see its results right here in front of you.

I originally invented a mood-tracking method to help me tame my own depression. Although it wasn't designed to be used by anyone other than me, people I knew started asking if they could try it out. So I turned it into an online tool called Moodscope that now supports many thousands of people, some saying it has saved their life. Moodscope has been recognized by the U.K. National Health Service and was voted #1 in a British government Department of Health poll.

It wasn't hard to find the motivation to write this book. I was passionate about it because I found it frustratingly difficult to get help when I battled with depression myself, so I had to learn the hard way how to support myself.

Now I want to help you overcome your own low mood without having to go through all the hoops I struggled with. You can start using *Nudge Your Way to Happiness* immediately, potentially beginning to see the difference as soon as tomorrow.

By working your way through the book you'll get to try 30 different practical happiness techniques, and because you'll be monitoring your progress as you go, you'll learn what works for *you*. Then, when you discover new ways of becoming happier, you can simply keep practicing them long-term. Low mood can have a devastating impact. Imagine being able to alter the course for us, for example. We're also aware that eating less of most things, but more vegetables and fruits, is desirable. In the same way that this empowers us to self-manage our physical health, shouldn't there be tools that enable us to maintain our mental health?

I think there should, and just as I did with Moodscope before, I've now applied myself to write and design this simple but powerful book.

Imagine what could happen when people with emotional health challenges who currently get no support can start to help themselves.

Imagine what could happen when young people struggling with low mood know there's a book like this that can offer them simple, practical help.

And imagine a world where people can start to manage their own mental well-being without having to wait for a sometimes ineffective system, or falling back on medication.

For a little book, this one has big ambitions.

Introduction

Of course you might have picked up this book out of casual interest, but it seems more likely to me that you've done so because your mood is low. Perhaps help seems hard to find?

In *Nudge Your Way to Happiness* I'll show you how you can take immediate small steps that are custom-designed to boost your mood. You'll monitor your progress as you go, so you'll actually see its results right here in front of you.

I originally invented a mood-tracking method to help me tame my own depression. Although it wasn't designed to be used by anyone other than me, people I knew started asking if they could try it out. So I turned it into an online tool called Moodscope that now supports many thousands of people, some saying it has saved their life. Moodscope has been recognized by the U.K. National Health Service and was voted #1 in a British government Department of Health poll.

It wasn't hard to find the motivation to write this book. I was passionate about it because I found it frustratingly difficult to get help when I battled with depression myself, so I had to learn the hard way how to support myself.

Now I want to help you overcome your own low mood without having to go through all the hoops I struggled with. You can start using *Nudge Your Way to Happiness* immediately, potentially beginning to see the difference as soon as tomorrow.

By working your way through the book you'll get to try 30 different practical happiness techniques, and because you'll be monitoring your progress as you go, you'll learn what works for *you*. Then, when you discover new ways of becoming happier, you can simply keep practicing them long-term. Low mood can have a devastating impact. Imagine being able to alter the course of your future.

I've successfully used all these techniques myself and, with the exception of a brief four-week period, have lived without needing antidepressants for over nine years.

Almost two-thirds of the people who tried out a prototype version of this book for only seven days substantially reduced their scores on a clinical depression test (see page 269).

By working your way through these pages you'll build new mood management skills and in just 30 days you should be happier than you are now.

It's true that people who have mild depression can often recover without treatment, but the average length of an episode is 6-8 months. If your doctor refers you to a therapist or psychiatrist, there can frequently be a waiting list. If he or she prescribes an antidepressant, those who experience a benefit (and certainly not *everyone* does) only start seeing it after 3-4 weeks.

But you can safely start working with this book *right now.*

Let's get started on nudging up your happiness score.

The techniques you're about to learn have proven results. Every single day for the next month you'll discover fresh secrets that can lift your mood immediately, *and* stay with you for the rest of your life.

Among many other revelations you'll discover how to stop yourself ruminating on bad days. You'll find out how to experience the mood-lifting effects of being out in nature even if things are so grim that you can't even step outside your front door. And you'll also learn how tidying up just one drawer could get your whole week off to a better start.

Follow the book's simple step-by-step suggestions, and it's entirely possible you'll change your life.

Why I Wrote This Book

In some ways I'd waited thirty years for that appointment at the local mental health clinic on a foggy December morning in 2006.

I was 50 and I'd enjoyed what many might say was a high-achieving life. There was the scholarship to study in the U.S.A. in my 20s. I started and ran a successful London advertising agency in my 30s, and had a late "gap year" traveling the world in my early 40s. Then in my 50s I'd co-founded a string of start-up businesses.

But it wasn't all that it seemed. Throughout those years I'd kept a big secret. Since my early 20s I'd struggled with depression. I don't want to over-dramatize things but at times I wondered how I made it through in one piece.

Somehow, though, I did—perhaps because the darkest days seemed punctuated with other periods of great energy, when ideas and creativity seemed to flow like water, helpful for someone doing my kind of work.

But as I grew older, things seemed to get worse. There were fewer good days and, it seemed, infinitely more bad ones. Adrian and Caroline, friends who had known me for 20 years, separately urged me to get help, so I arranged to see the local mental health specialists, and in due course I set off for that 2006 appointment.

To begin with I had reasonably high hopes. It seemed to me that if I had external confirmation that there was genuinely something wrong with me, surely it could be put right? After all, one way or another I'd been problem solving all my working life. Advertising is generally about finding a creative solution to your client's business challenge. More often than not, starting

3

any kind of business is about giving customers new answers to their old problems.

Unfortunately my initial optimism was misplaced. I sat with a woman who appeared to listen attentively as she took notes while I poured out my heart for 45 minutes. But then she closed her notebook and told me I needed to see a psychiatrist which, she explained belatedly, she wasn't.

What was she then? She hadn't really told me at the outset. Apparently her job was simply to assess people—to decide if they *really* needed help. Apparently she thought I did, but when I asked when this would be, she replied that it would probably be in about six weeks' time.

Six weeks.

She stood up to let me out of that dismal little secure psychiatric unit and I vividly remember walking home feeling a million times worse than I had when I arrived.

So much for getting help.

What now? Well, with the support of family and friends I scraped through the next month-and-a-half, including a challengingly unhappy Christmas, then finally returned to the same bleak building, *the following year*, but this time to see a proper psychiatrist, who was helpful and also horrified by what I told her about that first appointment.

The process of diagnosing a mental illness is pretty sketchy, to be honest. Based on what I told her in a single hour-long session, the psychiatrist said she could see I was indeed probably struggling with a depressive disorder.

Her proposal? "Come back in three months and tell us how you've been." I wouldn't see her personally again, she said, because staff in her position were on a rotation. However she assured me that her successor would soon pick things up from her notes, so would be able to suggest the appropriate kind of treatment or therapy.

Now at the time, this felt a reasonably satisfactory outcome, certainly better than that hopeless first appointment, so I headed home feeling fairly positive. But then on further reflection, dismay set in.

How on earth was I supposed to report back in three months without some way of recording how I'd been? The psychiatrist didn't ask me to keep a diary or track my symptoms. She offered me no tool or system. Not even a form to fill in.

Once again I was on my own. But fortunately this is where my creative skills kicked in.

Originally trained in graphic design, I was used to devising solutions to tricky problems, so I quickly got to work, turning a trusted, existing—but complex—mood test into a kind of simple card game I could "play" each morning to give myself a reliable mood score.

Tracking these scores on a graph, I suddenly started to feel more in control. If nothing else, I knew I could at least show this chart to the new psychiatrist.

Steadily, though, producing a picture of my ups and downs enabled me to begin to make sense of the fluctuations. For example, I noticed there often seemed to be modest lifts in my mood score the day after I'd spent time in the company of other people. As someone who believed himself to be pretty self-contained, perhaps even a bit introverted, this seemed odd. But the evidence was staring in my face. It clearly did me good to be around others.

Perhaps I should do more of it?

The trouble was, on my lowest days it was hard enough to leave home, let alone to contemplate socializing.

Curiously, the answer struck me when I went to see my doctor about headaches I'd been having.

After asking a few questions, he suggested I should return for a full neurological examination, which was duly arranged. Fortunately these tests showed I had nothing to worry about, but they made me realize that patients who tell their doctor they're getting headaches will receive a range of responses from "go home and take painkillers" to "don't move a muscle, I'm calling an ambulance".

Maybe I could apply a similar tailored approach to my need for human company? Perhaps I could do something modest on days when I felt really low, but something more ambitious when things were better?

And this is where the Buttercross Tearoom played a big part. It was in the park close to where I lived and worked.

Vince and Fil(omena), the couple who ran it, served up delicious homemade food, making it a fine place for lunch, and an ideal spot for an experiment. I figured that on my rough days, I'd go there and sit at a table on my own. I wouldn't really need to talk to anyone, but might benefit from simply having other people nearby. On better days, I'd chat to one or two of the other regular customers, or to Vince and Fil themselves. And on the very occasional day when I truly felt good, I'd make a conscious effort to pre-arrange to meet a friend there.

It sounds contrived, but this idea of giving myself one of three tailored "interventions" really did work.

I could get my dose of feeling connected to others, no matter how I was doing, and I'd see its effect when I recorded my mood the following morning.

It reminded me a little of those *Choose Your Own Adventure* books where the story takes different courses, on different pages, depending on your choices: "There are three doors in front of you. Which will you enter? Turn to page 21 if you choose the red door, page 26 if it's the blue one, or page 28 if you pick the green door."

I quickly saw that what worked for social connectivity might also apply to other mood-lifting activities.

It was a deeply important revelation. I realized I could take simple customized actions today, which could lift my mood tomorrow. It may seem blindingly obvious, but somehow when you're in the depths of despair you don't always think sensibly. Logic goes out of the window.

Knowing I wasn't a complete hostage to fortune—that I did in fact have the power to influence my own emotional state— was a tremendously powerful insight.

Three months after that second (better) appointment, I returned for a third. This time my reception was, frankly, bizarre. With my graph in my briefcase, I told the new psychiatrist I'd been working hard to track my mood and manage my depression myself.

He nearly went ballistic. I couldn't believe it. Crossing his arms sternly in front of him, he angrily accused me of behaving dangerously.

Huh? I thought I was just doing as I'd been asked, but this psychiatrist was having none of that. He complained that I was diagnosing myself, implying that patients simply can't be trusted to make sense of their own condition.

On the verge of standing up to leave, something made me

stop. I'd waited three months for this third appointment. Didn't I owe it to myself to at least show this indignant gentleman my graph? So I literally put my cards on the table, along with my charted scores.

Then things in the consulting room took an even more extraordinary turn.

"Where did you get these from?" he demanded, jabbing his finger at the cards. "From the internet?"

Goodness, now I was completely bewildered.

"Er, I made them."

"But did you get them from the internet?"

In retrospect this sounds hilarious, but at the time it was anything but. It felt as if the psychiatrist was determined to frame me as some kind of Google-scavenging nutcase. Somehow I persuaded him that the cards were entirely my idea, and that I'd actually—*honestly*—found them useful.

To be fair he did eventually soften his attitude a little, but the whole experience left me feeling that the U.K. mental health-care system: (a) couldn't really help people who were anything other than severely sick, and (b) seemed sold on the idea that the only way you could get help was from a professional.

Except, of course, that these professionals were all tied up with those with severe mental illness.

So the system didn't necessarily work. And when you look at the scale of the problem, you can understand why, at least to some extent.

You see, about one-in-four people will have a diagnosable mental illness in their lifetime. *One in four.* Sociologists estimate that the average individual knows about 150 people at least fairly well. So there are probably something like 37 people in your

reasonably close circle who'll get diagnosed with a mental illness. But of course things have to get pretty serious before
you're *formally* diagnosed. Millions struggle with more moderate emotional health problems, perhaps without ever asking for
assistance.

In fact large numbers of even those with *serious* mental illness fail to get help—the figure is more than 40% in the U.S.A.,
and even higher in the U.K. Often, stigma (real and perceived)
prevents people asking for the support they so badly need.

So we have a somewhat broken system, which in any case is
too small to cope with a huge problem that seems to be getting
even bigger. Not sounding good, is it?

I'm convinced my psychiatrist was incorrect to imply that
people cannot help themselves. I believe they can, especially if
they're given the right tools.

Unfortunately I can't really see the existing system developing them. It makes little business sense for the pharmaceutical
industry to explore non-medication treatments. At any given
time around one-in-ten adults are taking antidepressant medication, for example. A market this big represents massive profits
for drug manufacturers.

What's more, perhaps some of the more old-fashioned members of the psychiatric profession believe that only those within
their closed inner circle are capable of treating the mind. Their
argument might go something like this: You wouldn't carry out
heart surgery on yourself, so why would you consider do-it-
yourself mental health care? But I think this misses the point.
While it's obvious that no one should attempt a D.I.Y. coronary
bypass procedure, everyone can *and should* pay attention to
their heart health. We all know that brisk workouts can be good

for us, for example. We're also aware that eating less of most things, but more vegetables and fruits, is desirable. In the same way that this empowers us to self-manage our physical health, shouldn't there be tools that enable us to maintain our mental health?

I think there should, and just as I did with Moodscope before, I've now applied myself to write and design this simple but powerful book.

Imagine what could happen when people with emotional health challenges who currently get no support can start to help themselves.

Imagine what could happen when young people struggling with low mood know there's a book like this that can offer them simple, practical help.

And imagine a world where people can start to manage their own mental well-being without having to wait for a sometimes ineffective system, or falling back on medication.

For a little book, this one has big ambitions.

Quick Start Guide

Nudge Your Way to Happiness asks you to rate your mood once a day, and it's best to do this at the same time of day. You'll probably need around ten minutes, and in general first thing in the morning seems best for most people. Ready? Turn the page to see how it works.

For each of the 30 days of *Nudge Your Way to Happiness* you'll see a questionnaire page like the one shown on the right.

❶ Enter the date.

❷ Check one box in each of the ten rows of emotions and feelings that best reflects what you're experiencing at that moment.

❸ Add the scores by the boxes you've checked.

❹ Double that number to get your Well-being Score out of 100.

❺ Enter your score on the graph on pages 280 and 281.

❻ Write a few words that might help explain why you scored the way that you did.

❼ Go to the bottom right corner of the test page and your score will direct you to one of three tailor-made nudges.

The *Nudge Your Way* emotions and feelings defined:

ANGRY	Feeling furious
ANXIOUS	Being very concerned or worried
CHEERFUL	Having a happy outlook
HEALTHY	Having good physical health—not sick
IN PAIN	Feeling physical suffering or distress
LONELY	Feeling alone
LOVED	Feeling deep affection from others
MOTIVATED	Feeling driven to do things
TIRED	Being exhausted, fatigued, sleepy
UNDERSTOOD	Being accepted for who you are

How much are you experiencing these emotions and feelings right now?

Date: **August 26th, 2016** — **1**

	NOT AT ALL	VERY SLIGHTLY	A LITTLE	MODERATELY	QUITE A BIT	EXTREMELY
ANGRY	☐ 5	☑ 4	☐ 3	☐ 2	☐ 1	☐ 0
ANXIOUS	☐ 5	☐ 4	☑ 3	☐ 2	☐ 1	☐ 0
CHEERFUL	☐ 0	☐ 1	☐ 2	☑ 3	☐ 4	☐ 5
HEALTHY	☐ 0	☐ 1	☑ 2	☐ 3	☐ 4	☐ 5
IN PAIN	☐ 5	☐ 4	☐ 3	☐ 2	☑ 1	☐ 0
LONELY	☐ 5	☐ 4	☐ 3	☑ 2	☐ 1	☐ 0
LOVED	☐ 0	☐ 1	☑ 2	☐ 3	☐ 4	☐ 5
MOTIVATED	☐ 0	☐ 1	☐ 2	☑ 3	☐ 4	☐ 5
TIRED	☐ 5	☐ 4	☐ 3	☐ 2	☑ 1	☐ 0
UNDERSTOOD	☐ 0	☐ 1	☑ 2	☐ 3	☐ 4	☐ 5

2

Add numbers beside checked boxes – Total A: **23** — **3**

Multiply Total A x 2. This is your Well-being Score out of 100: **46** — **4**

Plot Well-being Score on graph on page 280, then... — **5**

...What happened? — **6**

Disagreement with Chris and still aching after too much garden work at weekend

Finally, if your score is...
0-42   Turn to Nudge 1C
43-67   Turn to Nudge 1A — **7**
68-100 Turn to Nudge 1B

1

Today you're putting one foot in front of the other to begin an important journey, and simply having the resolve to do this is worthy of congratulations.

How much are you experiencing these emotions and feelings right now?

Date: [ ]

	NOT AT ALL	VERY SLIGHTLY	A LITTLE	MODERATELY	QUITE A BIT	EXTREMELY
ANGRY	5	4	3	2	1	0
ANXIOUS	5	4	3	2	1	0
CHEERFUL	0	1	2	3	4	5
HEALTHY	0	1	2	3	4	5
IN PAIN	5	4	3	2	1	0
LONELY	5	4	3	2	1	0
LOVED	0	1	2	3	4	5
MOTIVATED	0	1	2	3	4	5
TIRED	5	4	3	2	1	0
UNDERSTOOD	0	1	2	3	4	5

Add numbers beside checked boxes – Total A: [ ]

Multiply Total A x 2. This is your Well-being Score out of 100: [ ]

Plot Well-being Score on graph on page 280, then...

...What happened?

Finally, if your score is...
0-42   Turn to Nudge 1C
43-67   Turn to Nudge 1A
68-100 Turn to Nudge 1B

When you have a bad spell it's common to believe it's always been this way, so don't despair if that's how you feel right now. It's a normal human reaction.

A helpful way of bouncing back is to recall previous mood-beating achievements, trying to recall what you did right in the past. That might not be easy, so your mission today is to enlist the help of a friend or family member who was around when you successfully fought back from a previous low.

Our minds sometimes protect us from past pain by blotting out unpleasant memories, so it could be that you can't even really remember what you did that helped.

And that's where others can lend a hand.

Reach out to someone whose memories might be more complete than your own.

Ask them to help you work out what made a difference, then plan to do the same kinds of things again soon.

Who has seen you recover from a low mood in the past?

....

How and when can you contact them?
E.g. By email this morning, in person tonight.

....

(Later.) What "bouncing back" strategies did they help you recall?

....

....

Who's got you covered?

Department stores sell few umbrellas on sunny days. When the weather's fine, people rarely plan for when it won't be.

In fact the same is often also true of our "emotional weather". If you're like me you probably don't think much about dealing with gloomy days when, for once, you're going through a better patch.

It's okay, it's human nature. But you know what? Right now, when things are better, it makes a lot of sense to invest in some contingency planning.

A useful way to bounce back from bad times is making sure you have one or two people you can count on, and I expect you know who they are.

I'm sure they'll do this unreservedly, probably as you would do for them if they needed support. But they're important to you, so why not reach out to them today?

Perhaps you have no need for their help right now, but you may in the future. And it's always easier to ask for support from someone who's known you in good times as well as bad.

Which one person has been there for you in the past, and probably will be again in the future?

....

How will you get in touch with them?
E.g. Email, phone calls, visit, greeting card

....

When can you schedule this?

....

Look on the bright side.

Pollyanna was the title character of a best-selling 1913 children's book of the same name. After her father taught her to play "The Glad Game" she became impossibly optimistic, always seeking the upside of the gloomiest situation.

For example, expecting to pull a doll from a lucky dip but finding instead a pair of crutches, Pollyanna's father told her to look on the bright side because, "We didn't need to use them!"

Although modern-day Pollyannas are derided for being unrealistic, I'd actually encourage you to adopt her mindset today to help change the way you view a current problem.

Begin by making up a "Pollyanna" view of the problem that's as ridiculous as possible. By all means laugh at yourself. But then gradually turn down the optimism control until you reach a point that's just about realistic and almost certainly more positive than your current one.

Tweaking the story is a great way to bounce back.

What's one current problem that's getting you down?
E.g. I'm afraid my low mood is going to make it impossible to go to work.

....

....

What would be a ridiculously optimistic way to view this issue?
E.g. Great! I'll hand in my notice and go live by the ocean!

....

How could this "Pollyanna" view reframe your problem?
E.g. Maybe I should ask my boss for a couple of days off to rest and recover.

....

....

2

You did the hard bit yesterday, starting your journey. It may help to refrain from thinking too hard about the process itself for now. Simply focus on making your time with the book a daily routine.

How much are you experiencing these emotions and feelings right now?

Date: [ ]

	NOT AT ALL	VERY SLIGHTLY	A LITTLE	MODERATELY	QUITE A BIT	EXTREMELY
ANGRY	5	4	3	2	1	0
ANXIOUS	5	4	3	2	1	0
CHEERFUL	0	1	2	3	4	5
HEALTHY	0	1	2	3	4	5
IN PAIN	5	4	3	2	1	0
LONELY	5	4	3	2	1	0
LOVED	0	1	2	3	4	5
MOTIVATED	0	1	2	3	4	5
TIRED	5	4	3	2	1	0
UNDERSTOOD	0	1	2	3	4	5

Add numbers beside checked boxes — Total A: [ ]

Multiply Total A x 2. This is your Well-being Score out of 100: [ ]

Plot Well-being Score on graph on page 280, then...

...What happened?

Finally, if your score is...
0-42   Turn to Nudge 2B
43-67   Turn to Nudge 2A
68-100   Turn to Nudge 2C

No more bananas.

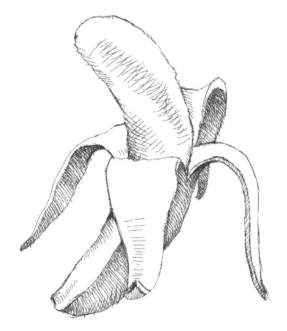

The term "comfort zone" has been in common use since the 1990s, but the idea of behaving in a way that minimizes stress and risk isn't exactly new.

Of course there are times when staying in your comfort zone makes sense. For example it probably stops you straying down dangerous dark alleys on the wrong side of town.

Sometimes, however, stepping out of your comfort zone can mean the difference between a so-so day and a truly memorable one. So let me recommend shaking up tried-and-tested routines a bit today.

A slightly unconventional way to pull this off is to take the last letter of the word that describes whatever you usually do, then decide to do something which begins with that letter instead.

Always eat a banan<u>A</u> for breakfast? Try an <u>A</u>pricot.

Generally watch the new<u>S</u> on TV? Why not try a <u>S</u>itcom?

While it's sensible not to disrupt behaviors you find genuinely comforting, it can be rewarding to introduce a little novelty now and then.

Which word describes a routine you could change?
E.g. Phone cal<u>L</u>, Sandwic<u>H</u>

....

Think of a new word that begins with the behavior's last letter.
E.g. <u>L</u>etter, <u>H</u>otdog

....

What can you do now to remind yourself to tackle things differently today?
E.g. Take out my writing paper, place a reminder in my wallet for lunchtime

....

....

Happily most zoos have changed, so it's rightly rare to find an animal kept in inhumane conditions these days.

But it wasn't always this way of course. Zoos of the past squeezed their animals into tiny cages, subjecting them to day-in, day-out routines that left them bored and hopeless. Just as you probably do, I shudder to think of it.

Oddly though, we humans sometimes incarcerate ourselves in imaginary cages of our own making, particularly when we feel low. Not surprisingly this makes us feel even worse.

By doing the same old thing in the same old way, day after day, we "cage ourselves," not even varying our surroundings. Please don't let that happen to you.

Today's a good day to shake things up just a little. Maybe you don't really feel like it, so tread lightly, but try to gently change some routines in the next 24 hours.

What do you do in the same way almost every day?
E.g. Always have the same thing for breakfast and eat it in the same place

....

How could you change the way you do this one thing?
E.g. Have fresh fruit instead of toast, take my breakfast into another room or the garden

....

(Later.) What was it like when you tried that?

....

....

In 1908 the psychologists Yerkes and Dodson explained that we perform better when our stress levels are slightly higher than normal.

They called this "Optimal Anxiety", suggesting that although too much stress is bad, just enough anxiety can be good for you.

How could you make use of this? Try stepping out of your comfort zone today. Not too far, but just enough to make you very slightly apprehensive.

Maybe you feel strong enough right now to try something a little different, so here are three suggestions.

How about pulling on an item of clothing you wouldn't usually wear?

Why not visit somewhere you've never been before (an art gallery, a cheese shop)?

Or take a completely new route and perhaps a different mode of transport for a journey you make every day?

Mix it up.

Do something that makes you feel just a little jittery.

What regular routine can you change in the next day?

....

How will you approach it differently?

....

In order to ensure you pull this off, what plans might you need to make?

....

....

3

With today's result you should now have three data points on your graph. It's early days but you may see the beginning of some kind of trend. Which way it goes doesn't matter too much to start with. You're doing well to keep the routine going.

How much are you experiencing these emotions and feelings right now?

Date: [_____]

	NOT AT ALL	VERY SLIGHTLY	A LITTLE	MODERATELY	QUITE A BIT	EXTREMELY
ANGRY	5	4	3	2	1	0
ANXIOUS	5	4	3	2	1	0
CHEERFUL	0	1	2	3	4	5
HEALTHY	0	1	2	3	4	5
IN PAIN	5	4	3	2	1	0
LONELY	5	4	3	2	1	0
LOVED	0	1	2	3	4	5
MOTIVATED	0	1	2	3	4	5
TIRED	5	4	3	2	1	0
UNDERSTOOD	0	1	2	3	4	5

Add numbers beside checked boxes – Total A: [_____]

Multiply Total A x 2. This is your Well-being Score out of 100: [_____]

Plot Well-being Score on graph on page 280, then...

...What happened?

Finally, if your score is...
0-42   Turn to Nudge 3C
43-67   Turn to Nudge 3B
68-100   Turn to Nudge 3A

Don't shut yourself away.

Imagine taking a dream vacation to somewhere you've always wanted to visit.

Everything's perfect.

The weather is superb. The hotel is magnificent. The location is even better than you'd dared hope.

So what do you do then? Well for some unknown reason, you spend the entire trip cooped up alone in your hotel room.

It makes no sense, does it? But this is not that different from feeling pretty good, as you do right now, only to bury yourself in electronic media.

There's a big, bright world out there waiting to be enjoyed, so why not take a complete break from technology today? Perhaps not for the whole day, but certainly make your break long enough to appreciate the calm stillness.

You may need to let others know so they don't worry about your electronic absence, but you'll almost certainly enjoy it.

When will you give yourself some time without technology?

....

What enjoyable activity can you plan instead?

....

Are you concerned about being without technology for a while? If so, record your worries below. Then forget them. I think you'll be fine.

....

....

One advantage of technology is that it can make you feel like you're never out of touch. If you need something or someone, it or they are only a button click away.

Unfortunately this state of constant connectivity can also leave you worrying that you'd miss something if you were without your electronic devices.

Perhaps instinctively you know that too much tech isn't good for you, but "FOMO" (Fear Of Missing Out) stops you from pushing the Off button.

I wouldn't mind betting though, that you do already turn your back on technology every night when you go to sleep. Then when you wake up six or seven hours later, guess what? That's right, the Internet is still there.

Sometime in the next 24 hours, therefore, I'd like to recommend that you unplug a little. Replace your use of technology with something that is better for you, even if only for a while.

When's a good moment to switch off electronic devices?
E.g. On my commute, two hours before bedtime

....

What will you do instead?
E.g. Tackle a crossword puzzle*, read a book

....

(Later.) How did that feel? Will you do it again?

....

....

*Er, not if your commute involves driving, of course.

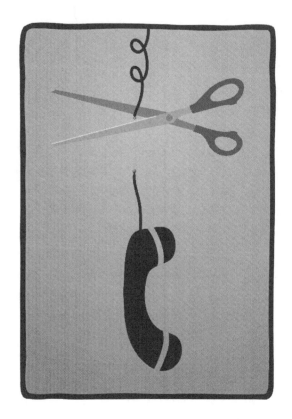

Take time out from tech.

In theory, technology should provide the ideal way to stay in touch with the world when your spirits are low. In theory. The reality is that when we feel a bit below par, most of us tend to shy away from tech-initiated contacts just as much as we do face-to-face connections.

Do you recognize this in yourself? The most you may do is check email and social media, but you could find yourself doing so incessantly. In fact, people suffering from low mood can end up feeling even worse because of social comparisons online: the "Everyone on Facebook is Having a Great Time, Except Me" syndrome.

If you're not feeling great, by all means pick up the phone to talk to a friend, or text them. But rather than waste hours becoming disillusioned on Facebook, why not take a healthy break from technology instead? Turn off the computer and TV, and go for a walk or curl up with a good book.

Of course, taking a tech break won't solve all your problems, but at the very least it might stop you from feeling worse. And at best you might even enjoy it.

Have you noticed yourself getting over-attached to technology, and if so, when?

E.g. Repetitively checking Facebook while also watching TV

....

When could you take a break from technology?

E.g. During the early evening, after dinner

....

What could you do to replace this?

E.g. Go for a walk around the block

....

....

4

Just as it helps to take medication at a fixed time every day, you could find it works best to record your scores with the book at the same time of day. Whenever that is, just make sure you'll have as few interruptions as possible.

How much are you experiencing these emotions and feelings right now?

Date: [   ]

	NOT AT ALL	VERY SLIGHTLY	A LITTLE	MODERATELY	QUITE A BIT	EXTREMELY
ANGRY	☐ 5	☐ 4	☐ 3	☐ 2	☐ 1	☐ 0
ANXIOUS	☐ 5	☐ 4	☐ 3	☐ 2	☐ 1	☐ 0
CHEERFUL	☐ 0	☐ 1	☐ 2	☐ 3	☐ 4	☐ 5
HEALTHY	☐ 0	☐ 1	☐ 2	☐ 3	☐ 4	☐ 5
IN PAIN	☐ 5	☐ 4	☐ 3	☐ 2	☐ 1	☐ 0
LONELY	☐ 5	☐ 4	☐ 3	☐ 2	☐ 1	☐ 0
LOVED	☐ 0	☐ 1	☐ 2	☐ 3	☐ 4	☐ 5
MOTIVATED	☐ 0	☐ 1	☐ 2	☐ 3	☐ 4	☐ 5
TIRED	☐ 5	☐ 4	☐ 3	☐ 2	☐ 1	☐ 0
UNDERSTOOD	☐ 0	☐ 1	☐ 2	☐ 3	☐ 4	☐ 5

Add numbers beside checked boxes – Total A: [   ]

Multiply Total A x 2. This is your Well-being Score out of 100: [   ]

Plot Well-being Score on graph on page 280, then...

...What happened?

Finally, if your score is...
0-42   Turn to Nudge 4C
43-67   Turn to Nudge 4A
68-100   Turn to Nudge 4B

Make your own morphine.

If you're like most people, I can't imagine you keep a supply of morphine and heroin in your medicine cabinet.

But even if you'd never dream of experimenting with narcotics, scientists suggest you may have already experienced a similar effect—through the simple act of helping someone else.

Altruistic behavior is known to raise the brain's own form of morphine- and heroin-like biochemicals, known as "endogenous opioids", producing a happy rush often referred to as the "helper's high".

However, don't simply take my word for it, try it for yourself. Why not plan a kindness day for the next 24 hours?

Taking part is simple. Just look for three opportunities to do nice things for people. Let someone go in front of you. Give someone a hug. Hold the door open.

Simple things. Big impact.

How could you plan to do your three kind things?
E.g. One on my journey to work, one at lunchtime, and another on the way home

....

....

On a scale of 0 to 5, how determined are you to do this?

....

(Later.) What, briefly, were the three kind things you did?

....

....

Be kind.

Feeling good can be contagious. When your mood is positive you're likely to "infect" other people. But even better, there's a way to "share the love" which may actually benefit you even more than those to whom you pass it on.

So what is it? Just be kind to people, and almost certainly you'll find no shortage of opportunities to help others in this way today.

In fact the Dalai Lama says: "Be kind whenever possible. It is always possible."

Here's an idea then.

As you go about your business today, imagine the Dalai Lama at your side, dressed in gold and maroon.

With every person you encounter, how might he suggest you react? What kindness would he encourage you to offer?

How much good could you do in one single day?

How can you remind yourself to channel your own inner Dalai Lama?

....

What do you think the Dalai Lama would say about your experiment?

....

....

(Later.) How did it feel to be kind to people?

....

....

Spell it out.

If you feel low, it's not unusual to feel uncared-for and unsupported.

Of course you're almost certainly viewing life through a distorting lens, but even though there are sure to be people who care about you and want to support you, it's common to feel abandoned when you're down.

Curiously, the best time to offer kindness to others is just when you feel you're receiving little yourself. You see, research suggests that we may actually get more out of helping other people than they do out of being helped.

Unfortunately it's hard to motivate yourself to behave kindly in a world that seems cruel. Maybe you could think of it as a kind of medication, though, and accept that—even when you know it's good for you—medicine often tastes bitter.

So look for opportunities to be kind to others today. Why not specifically make a point of thanking someone you notice doing a good job?

Set out to be kind today and—who knows?—maybe the world will return the compliment.

Where might you encounter someone doing a good job today?
E.g. On my way to work, at the grocery store

....

What's the smallest way in which you could pass on your thanks?
E.g. Simply saying "thanks for doing a good job" or even more simply, smiling.

....

....

How would you feel if someone praised you in the same way?

....

....

5

Some people are brought up to see books as precious objects, so the thought of writing in one may seem wrong. If that's the way you feel, though, think of this one as being like a diary or workbook. The more you put in it, the better it can help you.

How much are you experiencing these emotions and feelings right now?

Date: [   ]

	NOT AT ALL	VERY SLIGHTLY	A LITTLE	MODERATELY	QUITE A BIT	EXTREMELY
ANGRY	☐ 5	☐ 4	☐ 3	☐ 2	☐ 1	☐ 0
ANXIOUS	☐ 5	☐ 4	☐ 3	☐ 2	☐ 1	☐ 0
CHEERFUL	☐ 0	☐ 1	☐ 2	☐ 3	☐ 4	☐ 5
HEALTHY	☐ 0	☐ 1	☐ 2	☐ 3	☐ 4	☐ 5
IN PAIN	☐ 5	☐ 4	☐ 3	☐ 2	☐ 1	☐ 0
LONELY	☐ 5	☐ 4	☐ 3	☐ 2	☐ 1	☐ 0
LOVED	☐ 0	☐ 1	☐ 2	☐ 3	☐ 4	☐ 5
MOTIVATED	☐ 0	☐ 1	☐ 2	☐ 3	☐ 4	☐ 5
TIRED	☐ 5	☐ 4	☐ 3	☐ 2	☐ 1	☐ 0
UNDERSTOOD	☐ 0	☐ 1	☐ 2	☐ 3	☐ 4	☐ 5

Add numbers beside checked boxes – Total A: [   ]

Multiply Total A x 2. This is your Well-being Score out of 100: [   ]

Plot Well-being Score on graph on page 280, then

...What happened?

Finally, if your score is...
0-42   Turn to Nudge 5A
43-67   Turn to Nudge 5C
68-100   Turn to Nudge 5B

Photographic memories.

I'm sure we've both experienced that thing when you feel less shiny than usual and don't particularly want much to do with anyone.

This kind of "retreating to your cave" behavior is actually pretty common when people feel low, so neither of us should feel we're that unusual.

But maybe you know that your social connections play an important part in how you feel, so you end up in a kind of *Catch-22* situation. You recognize that connecting would probably help you feel better, but you don't want to connect because you feel bad.

But wait, there's good news, because researchers agree that the benefits of connection are actually linked to your subjective view of your relationships with others. So you may be able to "trick" your brain into feeling more connected without even picking up the phone.

One way to do that? Just take several minutes to look at photos of those closest to you. Gaze at them fondly, focusing on your warm connection. Try it. It can really work.

Which people do you wish you were more connected to right now?

....

Where can you find photos of them?

....

When can you spend five minutes looking at these pictures in real depth?

....

....

Tell them why they rock your world.

Here's a quiz question.

Which one of these four health conditions do you think poses the most risk? High blood pressure, lack of social connections, obesity, or smoking?

Remarkably, it's the second of these. Feeling lonely and unloved is a greater health threat than high blood pressure, obesity and smoking.

Right now you may feel relatively well-connected to others, but knowing how important it is to your future health, there's probably no better way to invest in your well-being than to spend a little time nurturing your relationships with those closest to you.

One simple but powerful way to do so is to tell them exactly why you care so much. Even if they look embarrassed, deep down they'll love to hear it.

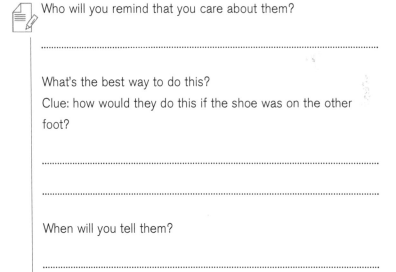

Who will you remind that you care about them?

....

What's the best way to do this?
Clue: how would they do this if the shoe was on the other foot?

....

....

When will you tell them?

....

....

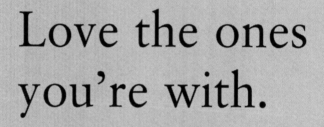

Based on the fact that social connections play an important part in whether we feel good or not, you might think supermarket clerks should be the happiest people in the world.

Just imagine how many people they must come into contact with every day.

So why do so many checkout operators look glum? Of course the truth is that it's not the *quantity* of connections you experience that counts, but their *quality*.

And the relationships that contribute most to your well-being are those that are close, secure and supportive. Fortunately you can boost the strength of these important connections whenever you wish, simply by nurturing your close relationships.

Today's a great day to do this. Someone somewhere will benefit from knowing you're thinking of them and caring about them. Let them know, and you'll feel closer.

A good feeling to have.

Who might need reminding that you care about them?

....

How can you get in touch with them?
E.g. Make a phone call, send an email or text, write a letter

....

When will you do this?

....

....

6

Sometimes psychotherapy clients find it hard to be honest in sessions, particularly at first. Perhaps they feel they'll be judged? You need have no such reservations while working with this book, so pour your heart out to its pages with no inhibitions. It's the best way.

How much are you experiencing these emotions and feelings right now?

Date:

	NOT AT ALL	VERY SLIGHTLY	A LITTLE	MODERATELY	QUITE A BIT	EXTREMELY
ANGRY	5	4	3	2	1	0
ANXIOUS	5	4	3	2	1	0
CHEERFUL	0	1	2	3	4	5
HEALTHY	0	1	2	3	4	5
IN PAIN	5	4	3	2	1	0
LONELY	5	4	3	2	1	0
LOVED	0	1	2	3	4	5
MOTIVATED	0	1	2	3	4	5
TIRED	5	4	3	2	1	0
UNDERSTOOD	0	1	2	3	4	5

Add numbers beside checked boxes – Total A:

Multiply Total A x 2. This is your Well-being Score out of 100:

Plot Well-being Score on graph on page 280, then

...What happened?

Finally, if your score is...
0-42   Turn to Nudge 6A
43-67   Turn to Nudge 6B
68-100 Turn to Nudge 6C

Happy snacks.

Why does sugar taste so good? Well, according to a Washington University study, it pretty much starts at birth. Newborns have a marked preference for sweet flavors, and this carries over into adult life.

Sadly, although nibbling sweet snacks may make us feel good, it's only for a while. The "sugar rush" is followed by a rapid crash as the insulin in your body tries to bring your blood glucose level back to normal.

Even though sweet snacks aren't a great way to get a hit when you feel low, many of us (me included) place temptation in our own way by stocking store cupboards with cakes, cookies, and other sugary foods "just in case".

When you feel low, it's common to get the munchies. Your body tells you to eat, but if the easiest snacks to eat are the sugary ones, you may end up bingeing on unhealthy food.

Prevent this by consciously putting snacks that will be better for you in the fridge, while moving less-healthy options to a shelf in a high cupboard.

Is it a trick? Yep. Can it work? Almost certainly.

Which healthy snacks do you enjoy?
E.g. Carrot sticks, nuts, fruit

....

Which unhealthy snacks do you reach for on difficult days?
E.g. Ice cream, cookies, cake

....

When can you stock up on the healthy stuff and hide the unhealthy?

....

....

Eat slowly and savor.

What you eat can have a big impact on your mood.

For example, consuming less sugar and fat, and eating more whole-grains, fruits, vegetables and legumes is likely to make you feel good.

But it's equally clear that *how* you eat is important, too. You see, even when things aren't especially bad emotionally, we may rush meals and multitask while we eat.

There's much to be said for making mealtimes more of an occasion, though. Make them mindful too.

Rather than crashing in front of the TV with your dinner piled in a bowl, why not (a) turn off the television, (b) serve up nicely arranged food on your best plate, and (c) take your time to enjoy and savor each mouthful?

Feeding your stomach is good. Why not feed your soul at the same time?

Which upcoming meal could become a mini feast rather than a drudge?

....

If it will involve others, who will you need to tell in advance?
E.g. "I'd love it if we sat down at the table together tonight"

....

What small additions could you make to heighten the sense of the occasion?
E.g. Light a candle, bring in a flower from the garden

....

....

Good for you.

Think about some of the ways that food takes center stage in celebrations. What would birthdays or weddings be like without a cake? How would Christmas feel minus the traditional lunch or dinner? Can you imagine Thanksgiving without pumpkin pie?

We probably have our ancient ancestors to thank for our tendency to put food at the center of important social gatherings. When they successfully hunted a wild animal, everyone celebrated by getting together to eat it.

You are of course at liberty to celebrate any time you wish—not only on high days and holidays. And what better reason to hang out the flags than feeling pretty good in yourself? What food could you mark this with? Doesn't it make sense to treat yourself to something tasty but healthy?

How about a delicious fresh fruit smoothie? Or a tasty piece of grilled salmon accompanied by a salad? Or a homemade pizza loaded with veggies and creamy mozzarella? Celebrate doing well with foods that make you feel even better.

What would make a delicious, healthy celebratory meal?

....

Is there someone to share it with? Celebrating alone
is perfectly fine, too, though.

....

When will you treat yourself?

....

....

7

After recording today's score, you'll have completed your first week with the book. You're about a quarter of the way through it. Maybe you'll see some kind of pattern or trend emerging. Great if you do, but fine if you don't. It's actually the process that counts at the moment.

How much are you experiencing these emotions and feelings right now?

Date: [   ]

	NOT AT ALL	VERY SLIGHTLY	A LITTLE	MODERATELY	QUITE A BIT	EXTREMELY
ANGRY	5	4	3	2	1	0
ANXIOUS	5	4	3	2	1	0
CHEERFUL	0	1	2	3	4	5
HEALTHY	0	1	2	3	4	5
IN PAIN	5	4	3	2	1	0
LONELY	5	4	3	2	1	0
LOVED	0	1	2	3	4	5
MOTIVATED	0	1	2	3	4	5
TIRED	5	4	3	2	1	0
UNDERSTOOD	0	1	2	3	4	5

Add numbers beside checked boxes – Total A: [   ]

Multiply Total A x 2. This is your Well-being Score out of 100: [   ]

Plot Well-being Score on graph on page 280, then

...What happened?

Finally, if your score is...
0-42   Turn to Nudge 7A
43-67   Turn to Nudge 7B
68-100 Turn to Nudge 7C

Leave the rumination to the cows.

Cows digest food in a peculiar way. They chew once, and then regurgitate some of it in order to do so a second time. I know. Yuck.

Sorry for the revolting description, but I draw attention to it to remind us that this process, called rumination, is kind of like the behavior of the same name that you and I may indulge in on a gray day.

In the thinking version of rumination, unhappy and unwanted thoughts go round and round in your head to the extent that it seems impossible to turn them off.

To be honest, it's very nearly as unpleasant as re-eating a partly-digested meal would be.

One helpful way to stop rumination, albeit temporarily, is to borrow from an approach everyone's talking about: mindfulness. Don't worry, it's not complicated. Literally all you have to do is spend five minutes truly observing your surroundings as if you were seeing them for the first time.

To do this, simply sit in a chair you don't normally occupy, then deeply and thoroughly notice what's around you, without judging in any way. Breathe slowly, noticing each breath.

You should notice yourself calming down. With luck you'll get a break from the rumination too.

Which seat will you sit in for your five minutes of taking notice?
Pick one you rarely occupy

....

When will you take this five minute break?
E.g. Right now, at lunchtime, after work

....

(Later.) What happened to your thoughts when you did this?

....

Notice everything.

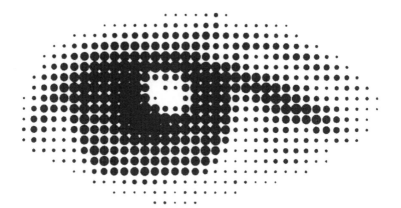

When you accuse someone of wearing blinkers, you're suggesting they're taking an overly-focused view of some or other situation rather than seeing the bigger picture.

Blinkers on horses are largely used for practical reasons of course. If a horse is working in a city street, for instance, you want it to focus on where it's going, rather than being distracted or spooked by what's behind or beside it.

On an average day most of us go through life pretty focused on what's in front of us, and that makes sense to some degree. We have things to do, places to go, people to see, so focus helps us get through our day.

But maybe it also prevents days being anything better than average.

A good tip for shifting thoughts beyond the everyday is to spend five minutes truly focusing on your environment.

And here's a way to do this even if you can't actually spare five minutes. Just build the process into something you're already doing.

An example? You could be doing the dishes or taking a shower. If it's the shower, for instance, pay full attention to the sensation of the water cascading onto your skin. Hear the sounds of the shower. Focus on the smell of the soap and shampoo.

Send other thoughts packing, and make the most of being in the moment.

Which normal activity can you turn into an opportunity to pay full attention to your surroundings?

....

When will you do this?

....

How do you think it will feel and (later) how did it feel?

....

....

Enjoy the small things.

Vivid colors frequently fulfill an important role in nature. The granular poison frog's bright red body, for example, acts as a signal to would-be predators that it tastes pretty noxious. The bright colors of flowers, on the other hand, attract pollinators.

Color also seems to play a part in human nature. I've often noticed—and perhaps you have too—that the world seems brighter and more vibrant on days when I feel good.

If this is your world right now, let's keep it that way, shall we? Maybe you're familiar with the principles of mindfulness, in which case you'll already know how to do what follows. If not, there's a way to sample its benefits very simply. And, by the way, those benefits can include managing pain, reducing blood pressure and possibly even boosting your immune system.

Here's how it works. Set aside ten minutes to sit comfortably with as few distractions as possible. Start by noticing your breathing, then as you slowly breathe in and out, study your surroundings in rich detail. Look at shapes, colors and textures. Notice any aromas. Listen to the sounds that drift into your ears. Feel the chair in which you sit.

There are whole books devoted to mindfulness, but just for now practice the easy version.

Drink in your surroundings without making judgment. Calm your mind. Notice everything. Enjoy.

When will you set aside 10 minutes for this easy mindfulness exercise?

....

Where will you do it?

....

(Later.) Well, how was it?

....

....

8

Turning to this book day after day takes determination and willpower, the same two attributes that can help you beat low mood. You're doing really well.

How much are you experiencing these emotions and feelings right now?

Date:

	NOT AT ALL	VERY SLIGHTLY	A LITTLE	MODERATELY	QUITE A BIT	EXTREMELY
ANGRY	5	4	3	2	1	0
ANXIOUS	5	4	3	2	1	0
CHEERFUL	0	1	2	3	4	5
HEALTHY	0	1	2	3	4	5
IN PAIN	5	4	3	2	1	0
LONELY	5	4	3	2	1	0
LOVED	0	1	2	3	4	5
MOTIVATED	0	1	2	3	4	5
TIRED	5	4	3	2	1	0
UNDERSTOOD	0	1	2	3	4	5

Add numbers beside checked boxes — Total A:

Multiply Total A x 2. This is your Well-being Score out of 100:

Plot Well-being Score on graph on page 280, then

...What happened?

Finally, if your score is...
0-42   Turn to Nudge 8A
43-67   Turn to Nudge 8C
68-100 Turn to Nudge 8B

Jigsaw peace.

Faced with the choice when you feel low, what's likely to do you most good: watching an hour of TV, or doing a jigsaw puzzle or crossword?

Psychologists would probably suggest that provided you really got into the jigsaw or crossword, an hour focused on activities such as these might help more than spending the same time in front of the TV.

If you're someone who enjoys puzzles, you may well find yourself getting "in the zone" with them—a state where you become so immersed in an activity that you lose all track of time. This is a concept known by psychologists as "flow". It can do wonders for your happiness levels.

But perhaps puzzles aren't your thing? No problem. Almost certainly you know what is. Maybe it's cooking or painting. It might be gardening or writing.

Flow activities tend to be enjoyable but challenging. Identifying what works for you makes sense today, as does finding time to immerse yourself in it.

What type of activity can put you "in the zone"?

....

How does it feel when you're in it?

....

When's the soonest you could schedule this activity?

....

....

Get in the zone.

If your car engine was running louder than usual it would probably be a sign that you're overdue for an oil change.

Oil changes are one of those tasks best seen as preventive maintenance.

It's a kind of "fix things before they need fixing" policy.

Could a similar idea apply to emotional well-being?

Absolutely.

It always makes sense to maintain your happiness levels in both good times (which you may be experiencing) and bad.

Of course it's not easy to motivate yourself to take action when you're already feeling okay. But what if the maintenance could leave you feeling even better?

One suggestion that could help you do exactly this is to spend time today in a state of "flow". It's what psychologists call the feeling of being so deeply immersed in whatever you're doing that you lose all track of time.

In terms of what works, it's different strokes for different folks, but you'll probably know your particular thing.

Is today a good day to experience flow?

You bet.

What's the thing that's most guaranteed to get you "in the zone"?

....

....

When can you schedule doing some of this?

....

Is there anything you need to prepare to make this possible? What is it? When will you make these preparations?

....

....

Forget what time it is.

Mihaly Csikszentmihalyi is an acclaimed psychologist with a famously complicated name, who has made it his life's work to study one particular psychological condition. You were very likely familiar with it at the age of nine.

As a child, I bet there was one activity that engaged you so thoroughly, so deeply, that you literally didn't hear your parents telling you to come to dinner.

Csikszentmihalyi called this state of mind "flow"—when you're so wrapped up in something (which needs to be enjoyable but also challenging) that you lose all track of time.

However, just like other things we naturally excelled at as children but have long since forgotten (drawing and handstands, for instance) you and I may now have to find "flow" in a more deliberate way.

Doing so makes sense, though. People who regularly spend time in this state tend to be psychologically healthier than those who don't.

My recommendation for the next 24 hours, then? Find a way to spend 30 minutes engrossed in something you're really good at. It could even be something on your To-Do list.

Bake a cake, frame a picture, mend the toaster. Where will you find flow?

What's something that needs doing, and can be done in such a way that you get "in the zone"?

....

When can you schedule this?

....

(Later.) So how did that feel?

....

....

9

Just like juggling, mood management is a skill, and just like juggling, the more you practice managing your mood, the better you'll get at it.

How much are you experiencing these emotions and feelings right now?

Date: [ ]

	NOT AT ALL	VERY SLIGHTLY	A LITTLE	MODERATELY	QUITE A BIT	EXTREMELY
ANGRY	5	4	3	2	1	0
ANXIOUS	5	4	3	2	1	0
CHEERFUL	0	1	2	3	4	5
HEALTHY	0	1	2	3	4	5
IN PAIN	5	4	3	2	1	0
LONELY	5	4	3	2	1	0
LOVED	0	1	2	3	4	5
MOTIVATED	0	1	2	3	4	5
TIRED	5	4	3	2	1	0
UNDERSTOOD	0	1	2	3	4	5

Add numbers beside checked boxes – Total A: [ ]

Multiply Total A x 2. This is your Well-being Score out of 100: [ ]

Plot Well-being Score on graph on page 280, then

...What happened?

Finally, if your score is...
0-42   Turn to Nudge 9B
43-67   Turn to Nudge 9C
68-100 Turn to Nudge 9A

Make it a day to remember.

In *Casablanca*, Humphrey Bogart's character Rick tells Ilsa (Ingrid Bergman) "We'll always have Paris", and in doing so he was, of course, being nostalgic.

Nostalgia can be a helpful way to fill your head with sunny thoughts on gloomy days, not that you feel this way right now, I suspect.

Dr. Constantine Sedikides is a psychologist at the University of Southampton who specializes in the field of nostalgia.

In his own life he seeks to create more moments that will be memorable.

"I don't miss an opportunity to build nostalgic-to-be memories," he says.

"We call this anticipatory nostalgia."

Although it may seem far-fetched or contrived to actively attempt to create memories that will become nostalgic in the future, there's certainly a lot to be said for living life to the fullest—and no harm whatsoever in heading into the next 24 hours with at least the possibility of this becoming a day to remember.

What might make the coming day truly memorable?

....

What would need to happen to make this so?

....

What plans could you hatch to make this at least a possibility?

....

....

A blast from your past.

It used to be thought that living in the past was an unhealthy preoccupation, emotionally speaking. But over the last 15 years, psychologists have increasingly recognized that a certain amount of nostalgia can be good for you.

The key to avoiding it assuming a negative flavor seems to be to steer clear of making comparisons between then and now. Instead, whenever you need a boost, simply enjoy happy memories from the past.

One effective way to fast-track your journey back to more positive times is to play music from that era. In fact music is a favorite tool of psychology researchers who for one reason or another want to induce nostalgia as part of an experiment.

There are YouTube videos containing mixes of hits from most years, but my recommendation is that you just listen to the music rather than watching the videos. The images you create in your mind will almost certainly be far more vivid, far more relevant, than those on YouTube. Ready? Let's go back in time.

What was a happy age for you?

Work out the year by adding this age to your year of birth

....

When can you schedule a short burst of time travel via music?

....

(Later.) How was it?

....

....

Reminisce.

Nostalgia, runs the old joke, isn't what it used to be.

And thank goodness for that, actually.

A Swiss doctor coined the term nostalgia in the 17th century to describe a neurological disease he said was of "essentially demonic cause".

Bizarrely, military doctors speculated that its occurrence among Swiss mercenaries fighting abroad was due to earlier damage to the soldiers' brain cells caused by the incessant clanging of cowbells in the Alps.

These days, psychologists agree that a reasonable amount of nostalgia—looking back fondly at happier times in the past—can be psychologically beneficial.

So why not deliberately set out to enjoy some nostalgic thoughts in the next 24 hours? Maybe you can do that in a phone call to an old friend? Tell them you were thinking about them, and that in particular you were recalling their part in a happy memory of the past.

Discuss it, and enjoy your joint reminiscences.

Which old friend springs to mind when you recall happy times?

....

What event is this friend most associated with?

....

How can you get in touch with them? When will you do so?

....

....

10

19th century engineer Lord Kelvin said, "If you can not measure it, you can not improve it." He wasn't talking about mood of course, but what if the same principle could apply to both engineering and happiness?

How much are you experiencing these emotions and feelings right now?

Date:

	NOT AT ALL	VERY SLIGHTLY	A LITTLE	MODERATELY	QUITE A BIT	EXTREMELY
ANGRY	5	4	3	2	1	0
ANXIOUS	5	4	3	2	1	0
CHEERFUL	0	1	2	3	4	5
HEALTHY	0	1	2	3	4	5
IN PAIN	5	4	3	2	1	0
LONELY	5	4	3	2	1	0
LOVED	0	1	2	3	4	5
MOTIVATED	0	1	2	3	4	5
TIRED	5	4	3	2	1	0
UNDERSTOOD	0	1	2	3	4	5

Add numbers beside checked boxes — Total A:

Multiply Total A x 2. This is your Well-being Score out of 100:

Plot Well-being Score on graph on page 280, then

...What happened?

Finally, if your score is...
0-42   Turn to Nudge 10B
43-67   Turn to Nudge 10C
68-100 Turn to Nudge 10A

Get to the bottom of something.

I'm not sure I completely agree with the suggestion that your school days are the happiest of your life. Although I have fond memories of having a certain amount of fun, I'm pretty sure I also experienced a certain amount of dismay.

Well at least I had a balanced education.

One thing I do recall, though, is the unadulterated joy of discovering something new and exciting that I couldn't wait to share with others. When you learn something new as a kid, you believe you're the first person in civilization to discover it.

No doubt about it, learning can be rewarding. Unfortunately we sometimes "unlearn" (forget) this.

So why is learning good for you? Well, not only does it give you a sense of achievement, it can boost your self-confidence.

When you're enjoying a good spell, it can be easy to forget the importance of doing things that will help you keep that way. Please don't. Try to add some learning to your day as a way to maintain your current state of well-being.

Here's a simple suggestion. Learning is best when it's a bit challenging, so why not set yourself the goal of teaching yourself the meaning of some idea that's been bugging you? It could be something from the news, a concept you've read about, or an idea someone's passed on without proper explanation. Now's the time to engage in some detective work.

What's something you've heard about, but don't fully understand?

E.g. Arab Spring, Cognitive Behavioral Therapy, Paleo Diet

....

How could you learn more about this?
E.g. Online, visiting the library, asking a friend

....

When will you do this?

....

....

Take a reading adventure.

People who continue to learn as their life progresses say it increases their ability to cope with stress, and that it also gives them greater self-confidence. Those were some of the findings of a 2004 University of London study that also showed that learners report higher self-esteem.

Doesn't that seem as if it could help someone going through a spell where their mood is lower than normal?

You're hardly likely to enroll for some kind of formal educational program when your mood isn't great, of course. But we shouldn't let this stop us applying the broad idea that learning something new can be good for our emotional well-being.

Psychologists suggest it's best to make this learning somewhat challenging, and a remarkably easy way to get outside your comfort zone while you go on a mini voyage of discovery is to find yourself a copy of a magazine you'd generally never imagine reading—either a hard copy, or an online version.

Choose a subject area that interests you but of which you have only sketchy knowledge, and then challenge yourself to find out three things you didn't previously know. Make a note of them below and you'll very likely be giving yourself a lift without even knowing it.

What subject matter interests you sufficiently to look at a magazine that's a little outside your comfort zone?
E.g. Archaeology, zoology

....

Where can you get access to a magazine on this subject?
E.g. Bookstore, library, online

....

(Later.) What three things did you learn?

1. ....

2. ....

3. ....

Mending, cleaning, learning.

"Lifelong learning is like a health club for your brain," suggests Nancy Merz Nordstrom, an educational expert from New Hampshire.

I think she's right. People who keep learning tend to report higher self-esteem, self-confidence, hope and purpose. They also say they're better at coping with stress. So why doesn't everyone just learn every day then, if doing so means they'd benefit from well-being boosts like these?

One problem is time. When your life is busy, you probably don't have enough of it to sign up for formal classes.

This would be like paying for a health club subscription but never showing up.

However, just as you might solve the health club challenge by building exercise into your daily life instead of going to a gym, why not find ways to build learning into the things you already do every day?

Here's an idea. I wouldn't mind betting there's something in your home that needs fixing or cleaning. All the better if you've put off tackling it because you think it'll be a tricky task. The emotional benefits of learning are greatest when you have to challenge yourself. So fear not.

Find out online how to handle the project, and then give yourself a boost by actually completing it.

Just make sure you pick something you can reasonably pull off, though.

Rewiring the whole house might not fall into that category.

What's broken or dirty that you could fix or clean?

....

When can you spend 10 minutes teaching yourself how to do this?

....

And when can you schedule time to carry out the repair or cleaning task?

....

....

11

Pausing to reflect, as you are by working through this book, is a helpful habit to develop. Taking a little time every day to evaluate life can leave you feeling more in control.

How much are you experiencing these emotions and feelings right now?

Date: [   ]

	NOT AT ALL	VERY SLIGHTLY	A LITTLE	MODERATELY	QUITE A BIT	EXTREMELY
ANGRY	5	4	3	2	1	0
ANXIOUS	5	4	3	2	1	0
CHEERFUL	0	1	2	3	4	5
HEALTHY	0	1	2	3	4	5
IN PAIN	5	4	3	2	1	0
LONELY	5	4	3	2	1	0
LOVED	0	1	2	3	4	5
MOTIVATED	0	1	2	3	4	5
TIRED	5	4	3	2	1	0
UNDERSTOOD	0	1	2	3	4	5

Add numbers beside checked boxes – Total A: [   ]

Multiply Total A x 2. This is your Well-being Score out of 100: [   ]

Plot Well-being Score on graph on page 280, then

...What happened?

Finally, if your score is...
0-42   Turn to Nudge 11C
43-67   Turn to Nudge 11A
68-100   Turn to Nudge 11B

Walk a mile, wear a smile.

Richard Wiseman began his career as a professional magician, but he's now Britain's only professor for the public understanding of psychology. In his 2012 book *Rip It Up* (later retitled *The As If Principle* in the US) he explained the ideas of

19th-century psychologist William James, who suggested that while people had always assumed emotions drive our behaviors (we run away from a bear because we are scared of it) it may actually be the other way around (we become scared because we're running away from the bear).

In fact, modern research backs up James, and Richard Wiseman proposes many ways in which you and I can use James's ideas ourselves. He says we can change the way we feel by acting "as if" we already feel that way.

Psychologist James D. Laird proved, for example, that "making" yourself smile can actually cause you to become happier. So here's a suggestion. Wear a deliberate smile on your face next time you take a walk, and all the better if your route takes you past other people. Even if this makes you feel conspicuous, you'll probably catch one or two of them smiling back, whether or not you actually directly look at each other.

When can you take a walk and experiment with smiling?

....

Practice the smile now. Make it wide and raise your eyebrows slightly. Write "Done!" below when you're finished.

....

(Later.) How did it feel when you smiled as you walked? Did anyone smile back?

....

....

Make a fist, change a habit.

There's a well-accepted principle in psychology that's best summed up by the idea of acting "as if".

An example? In a simple experiment, participants were

asked either to clench a pen lightly between their teeth, creating a smile, or to place one end of the pen in their mouth pointing straight out, leading to something approximating a frown.

It may sound simplistic, but when the participants' mood levels were subsequently checked, the smilers had become happier than the frowners.

As you seem to be doing pretty well right now, you probably have no need to "fake it until you make it" in terms of happiness. However you could still apply the technique for another reason.

Since you're probably feeling relatively strong, perhaps you're aiming to make some kind of habit change?

Maybe changing your diet, or aiming for more exercise, for example?

Lifestyle changes like these often depend on willpower, and Iris Hung from the National University of Singapore showed that you can "induce" willpower by making your hand into a fist. So if you're trying to avoid the cookie jar, try scrunching up your hand.

Is there something you'd like to change which requires willpower? If so, what is it?

....

When's the next time you may need to create a fist?

....

(Later.) What happened? Did it help?

....

....

Fake it to make it.

William James, brother of the novelist Henry James, is regarded by many as the first psychologist, working at Harvard University in the late 19th century.

Present-day psychologists have told me that he was way ahead of his time, one example being an idea of his that we might nowadays call "fake it until you make it".

Before James, most experts believed our emotions drive our behaviors. You're happy, so you smile.

But James was convinced that the relationship was more of a two-way street.

For example he said that if you persuade someone to form their face into a smile, they'll actually become happier.

In fact, this idea has been proved in recent research.

Now, on a day when you may be feeling below par, it's unlikely that you'll find it within you to force a fake smile.

Here's a useful technique you may like to try, however.

Simply watch a video of something you find genuinely amusing, perhaps on YouTube, deliberately pushing yourself to laugh and smile in an accentuated way.

Play the part of an amused audience member, if you like.

If you feel slightly happier as a result (and you may) it could well be because you acted "as if", and therefore became what you pretended to be.

What funny video is almost guaranteed to amuse you?

....

When can you watch it, perhaps on YouTube?

....

(Later.) How did that make you feel?

....

....

12

When your score dips, ask yourself if there was a cause. If so, can you prevent whatever it was from happening again in the future?

How much are you experiencing these emotions and feelings right now?

Date: [   ]

	NOT AT ALL	VERY SLIGHTLY	A LITTLE	MODERATELY	QUITE A BIT	EXTREMELY
ANGRY	5	4	3	2	1	0
ANXIOUS	5	4	3	2	1	0
CHEERFUL	0	1	2	3	4	5
HEALTHY	0	1	2	3	4	5
IN PAIN	5	4	3	2	1	0
LONELY	5	4	3	2	1	0
LOVED	0	1	2	3	4	5
MOTIVATED	0	1	2	3	4	5
TIRED	5	4	3	2	1	0
UNDERSTOOD	0	1	2	3	4	5

Add numbers beside checked boxes – Total A: [   ]

Multiply Total A x 2. This is your Well-being Score out of 100: [   ]

Plot Well-being Score on graph on page 280, then

...What happened?

Finally, if your score is...
0-42   Turn to Nudge 12C
43-67   Turn to Nudge 12B
68-100 Turn to Nudge 12A

Set an alarm for bed time.

An important part of looking after yourself is making sure you get a good night's sleep. I'm sure you know how refreshing it can be to wake up after a great night, but also how irritable you may feel after a restless sleep.

When you feel pretty good, as may be the case at the moment, you might be tempted to stay up later than usual.

But at the risk of sounding like a party pooper, it's actually sensible to have a reasonably strict discipline about the time you go to bed and get up, even on weekends.

So here's an idea that could make it easier to get to bed at a fixed time.

You may already set an alarm to wake you in the morning, but what about another to remind you of bedtime?

This can avoid that situation where you sit in front of the TV oblivious to the passage of time.

Although you're likely to be in good shape at the moment, please remember how helpful it can be to get a night's sleep.

Chronic insomnia can increase an individual's risk of suffering from a mood disorder.

For instance, people with insomnia are five times more likely to develop depression.

So why not set that alarm, if only to be on the safe side?

What time should you head for bed tonight?

....

How could you set an alarm to remind yourself?
E.g. On my phone

....

Start your night right.

A good night's sleep can make an amazing difference to your mood and overall well-being.

But however well you're sleeping at the moment, I'd like to suggest an idea that may do you good.

You know the way fancy hotels offer a turndown service?

The housekeeper visits your room during the evening to prepare your bed.

Well, I'd like to propose you do this for yourself.

About an hour before bedtime tonight, turn down the covers and plump the pillows. You could even put a "Sleep Tight" or "Sweet Dreams" note on the pillow, and perhaps leave yourself a glass of milk and a small plate of cookies.

Milk contains tryptophan, an amino acid that the body cleverly converts to serotonin and melatonin, the brain's natural relaxation chemicals.

Provide your own turndown service tonight, then. Cheesy? Perhaps. Effective? Quite probably. Fun? Unquestionably.

How would you prepare the bed of someone really special?
E.g. Flowers, chocolate, cookies, scent.

....

Wouldn't you agree you're rather special?

....

What time will you do your turndown service tonight?
E.g. An hour before bedtime.

....

....

How are you sleeping?

I know from my own experience that it's not unusual to have sleep problems when you feel a bit shabby.

Some people sleep too much, while others (my case) toss and turn with insomnia.

Although it's unpleasant, it's not uncommon. So you're not alone if you're currently having sleep problems.

The strange thing is, although scientists know insomnia and depression often occur together, it's a chicken-and-egg thing.

Depression could cause insomnia, or lack of sleep might play a contributory part in the onset of depression.

Nobody really knows.

But one thing's clear. Lack of sleep often leads to irritability and short temper, and makes you vulnerable to stress.

If your sleep is poor right now, you may find yourself ruminating about problems while you lay awake.

One way to deal with spiraling negative thoughts is to leave a pen and paper beside your bed at night so you can keep a kind of "Worry Journal".

Write down your worries, and then tell yourself that you've "parked" them for the time being.

Are you finding it less easy to sleep at the moment?
Are you lying awake turning thoughts over and over?

....

Do you think it could help to start a Worry Journal that you could leave by the bed?

....

When could you organize this?

....

....

13

Congratulate yourself when your score rises. Try to pin down why it did so, and then try to create the same conditions again on other days.

How much are you experiencing these emotions and feelings right now?

Date: [   ]

	NOT AT ALL	VERY SLIGHTLY	A LITTLE	MODERATELY	QUITE A BIT	EXTREMELY
ANGRY	☐ 5	☐ 4	☐ 3	☐ 2	☐ 1	☐ 0
ANXIOUS	☐ 5	☐ 4	☐ 3	☐ 2	☐ 1	☐ 0
CHEERFUL	☐ 0	☐ 1	☐ 2	☐ 3	☐ 4	☐ 5
HEALTHY	☐ 0	☐ 1	☐ 2	☐ 3	☐ 4	☐ 5
IN PAIN	☐ 5	☐ 4	☐ 3	☐ 2	☐ 1	☐ 0
LONELY	☐ 5	☐ 4	☐ 3	☐ 2	☐ 1	☐ 0
LOVED	☐ 0	☐ 1	☐ 2	☐ 3	☐ 4	☐ 5
MOTIVATED	☐ 0	☐ 1	☐ 2	☐ 3	☐ 4	☐ 5
TIRED	☐ 5	☐ 4	☐ 3	☐ 2	☐ 1	☐ 0
UNDERSTOOD	☐ 0	☐ 1	☐ 2	☐ 3	☐ 4	☐ 5

Add numbers beside checked boxes − Total A: [   ]

Multiply Total A x 2. This is your Well-being Score out of 100: [   ]

Plot Well-being Score on graph on page 280, then

...What happened?

Finally, if your score is...
0-42   Turn to Nudge 13B
43-67   Turn to Nudge 13C
68-100 Turn to Nudge 13A

Can you make it fun to exercise?

Making changes to routines isn't easy when you feel low, but since things seem reasonably good for you right now, how about making the most of the opportunity to set some well-being wheels in motion? For instance, why not think about making a gentle adjustment to the amount of physical exercise you get?

The relationship between exercise and mood is pretty incontrovertible, and what seems most important is staying fairly active every day rather than getting a boatload of strenuous exercise less regularly.

The best results seem to come from doing a little each day.

If you're already sufficiently active, great, keep it up. But if you're not, it makes sense to aim for 20 or 30 minutes of moderate activity such as walking every day.

Perhaps you feel you won't enjoy it? If you hope to maintain it, getting something out of your exercise regime is important. Achieve this by walking somewhere you'll enjoy—to visit a friend, or to the coffee shop, say. Or walk as part of your daily routine—go on foot rather than taking the bus. Another idea is to listen to an audiobook or to your favorite music. Some people like to call a friend or relative as they walk.

Today's a fine day to think about getting more exercise.

What type of exercise could fit into your daily routine without too much trouble?

....

How can you make this exercise more enjoyable?
E.g. Listen to music, stop in to see a friend

....

When could you begin this new routine? Today? Tomorrow?

....

....

Get very slightly active.

If I told you there was a simple action you could probably take right now which would have a beneficial effect on your mood within, say, five minutes, I'm guessing you might well be interested?

But if I went on to explain that this action is that you should do some physical exercise, I suspect you'd shrug and dismiss my suggestion.

Even though we know exercise can make us feel good, it's hard to find the motivation to get active when you have a case of the blahs. But that's almost as bad as not taking aspirin when you have a headache.

Wait though, there's good news. You see, the mood-lifting effects of exercise can kick in pretty quickly. Even a modest amount of activity will get the ball rolling. A brisk ten minute walk can do the trick, for instance.

Actually a short neighborhood walk could be just the thing. You might even exchange smiles or brief greetings with other people, giving you the double whammy of a little exercise combined with a small amount of social contact. Connecting with people is another way to help lift your spirits.

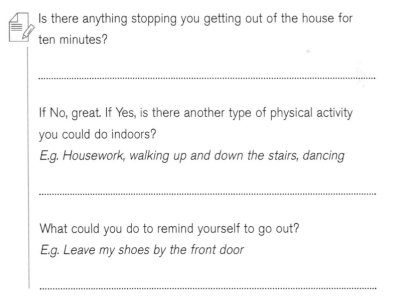

Is there anything stopping you getting out of the house for ten minutes?

....

If No, great. If Yes, is there another type of physical activity you could do indoors?
E.g. Housework, walking up and down the stairs, dancing

....

What could you do to remind yourself to go out?
E.g. Leave my shoes by the front door

....

Exercise needn't be complicated.

Taking care of your body is a great way to also take care of your mind, and one means of doing this is to keep physically active. Exercise causes your body to release chemicals known as endorphins, which interact with your brain to reduce awareness of pain. They can also trigger a positive euphoric feeling something similar to that produced by morphine. Just imagine, a legal high, no side effects, and all manufactured by your body.

The trouble is, it can be hard to get started with exercise simply because it all seems complicated. Joining the gym and finding the right clothing can be time consuming and expensive.

Fortunately help is at hand, though. There are many varieties of moderate exercise that can help with low mood, including aerobics, cycling, dancing, gardening, housework, swimming, and walking. Even cleaning the car can count.

So pick something you think you'll enjoy, and make it an activity you can do right away rather than something you'll put off until tomorrow.

What type of physical activity do you enjoy?

....

What's an example of a physical activity in the past that gave you a buzz?

....

Knowing this, what physical activity can you schedule for the coming 24 hours?

....

....

14

Daily routines can play a big part in supporting emotional health, and a daily routine is at least one component of what you're achieving by working your way through the book.

How much are you experiencing these emotions and feelings right now?

Date:

	NOT AT ALL	VERY SLIGHTLY	A LITTLE	MODERATELY	QUITE A BIT	EXTREMELY
ANGRY	5	4	3	2	1	0
ANXIOUS	5	4	3	2	1	0
CHEERFUL	0	1	2	3	4	5
HEALTHY	0	1	2	3	4	5
IN PAIN	5	4	3	2	1	0
LONELY	5	4	3	2	1	0
LOVED	0	1	2	3	4	5
MOTIVATED	0	1	2	3	4	5
TIRED	5	4	3	2	1	0
UNDERSTOOD	0	1	2	3	4	5

Add numbers beside checked boxes — Total A:

Multiply Total A x 2. This is your Well-being Score out of 100:

Plot Well-being Score on graph on page 280, then

...What happened?

Finally, if your score is...
0-42   Turn to Nudge 14A
43-67   Turn to Nudge 14C
68-100 Turn to Nudge 14B

Bring the outdoors indoors.

Take most dogs outdoors and they'll spring to life, even more so when the leash is slipped off, allowing them to race around like the wild creatures they evolved from. The majority of animals—humans included—thrive in nature.

Although you may not be up to exploring right now, I'm sure you'll recall times in the past when you felt good in the countryside or wilderness.

Fortunately it's possible to experience at least some of nature's restorative effects without setting foot outside your front door.

Here are three suggestions.

(1) Place a green-leaved plant on your desk or somewhere in your line of sight. Even better if it has a fragrance. Basil or lavender are examples.

(2) Some experts suggest that watching a nature film, or looking at pictures of wildlife and beautiful environments can help.

(3) Lastly, don't forget sounds. Search YouTube for "natural sounds" to bring birdsong, waves or waterfalls into your living room.

What could you do to bring a taste of nature into your home?
E.g. Get a plant, watch a video, play natural sounds

....

....

When can you experiment with this idea?

....

....

When I reflect on my life, I see that some of my happiest moments have been when I was in Big Nature. Mountains, oceans, and forests have always cheered me up.

As a matter of fact, you and I have probably been programmed to benefit from the healing powers of the natural world. Evolution moves at a snail's pace, and in these terms it's really not long since our early ancestors spent their entire lives outdoors.

We would do well to remember this when we spend our own days hermetically sealed in the homes, offices and cars that may actually be keeping us insulated from what's good for us.

Although Big Nature is best, any nature is good for you, to be honest. So here's my suggestion. Almost certainly there's some green space close by right now.

Open up Google Maps, search for your current location, and then look for a light green patch nearby—even better if it's somewhere new to you.

Head there at lunchtime, or whenever you can, then (and this is important) find somewhere comfortable to sit so you can properly observe your surroundings using all your senses.

There's nature out there, and it's not far away. Enjoy.

Where is the closest green space on Google Maps?

....

When will you explore it?
E.g. Lunchtime, tomorrow

....

(Later.) How did it go?

....

....

Hello sunshine.

One simple way to boost your well-being is to spend time outdoors, even more so if you can get out into nature.

Now, there are plenty of theories about why we find nature so restorative, but among the more interesting is the idea that the natural world's vivid colors may cause our brains to work harder in order to process all that visual information, distracting us from our cares and worries.

Another outdoor boost comes in the shape of the Vitamin D produced by our bodies when skin is exposed to sunlight.

Although diminished, it even works on overcast days.

While Big Nature is best, there are benefits to be had from the smallest exposure.

For instance, going for a walk and noticing tiny plants sprouting out of pavement cracks can work.

The key is to observe in as much detail as possible, paying the sort of attention our amazing natural world deserves.

When's the next time you can get outdoors for a walk?

....

Where will you go?

....

....

If preparations are needed, what are they, and when will you make them?

....

....

15

You're exactly half-way through the book today, so there's just as much behind you as there is in front of you now. Look back at where you've come from, and ahead at where you're going.

How much are you experiencing these emotions and feelings right now?

Date: [   ]

	NOT AT ALL	VERY SLIGHTLY	A LITTLE	MODERATELY	QUITE A BIT	EXTREMELY
ANGRY	5	4	3	2	1	0
ANXIOUS	5	4	3	2	1	0
CHEERFUL	0	1	2	3	4	5
HEALTHY	0	1	2	3	4	5
IN PAIN	5	4	3	2	1	0
LONELY	5	4	3	2	1	0
LOVED	0	1	2	3	4	5
MOTIVATED	0	1	2	3	4	5
TIRED	5	4	3	2	1	0
UNDERSTOOD	0	1	2	3	4	5

Add numbers beside checked boxes — Total A: [   ]

Multiply Total A x 2. This is your Well-being Score out of 100: [   ]

Plot Well-being Score on graph on page 280, then

...What happened?

Finally, if your score is...
0-42   Turn to Nudge 15B
43-67   Turn to Nudge 15C
68-100 Turn to Nudge 15A

If I get a cold, I always hope I won't pass it on to others, trying to convince myself through some strange, twisted logic that I'm not contagious. Oddly, a similar kind of thinking applies to my moods, as I often forget that emotions can actually be pretty contagious.

When you're around positive people, some of their energy rubs off onto you, but the opposite is true when you spend time with grumpy, negative individuals. Without really knowing it, you may pick up some of their lowness.

Since you're probably doing quite well at the moment, should you avoid people who aren't equally buoyant? Well, no. That's probably both impractical and insensitive.

In fact, when you're going through a better spell you may have the strength to support someone who isn't, and the act of helping can also give you a boost.

But how do you spend time with someone in low spirits without being pulled down yourself? Research has shown it's possible to pull this off by remaining slightly disassociated from the problem, while sympathizing with the person you're helping. Do so by imagining you're watching them on a TV show.

It's a technique used by people in the caring professions to avoid "burnout"—being unable to do your job because you've become overloaded by taking on others' problems.

Maybe you'll find it useful in the next 24 hours.

Who might need your emotional support at the moment?

....

How could you remind yourself to disassociate when you're supporting them?

....

....

How and when can you make contact with them?

....

....

Who could infect you with happiness?

Is low mood contagious? Can you "catch it"? Surprisingly the answer, to some degree, is yes.

Psychologists call the effect "emotional contagion", and it tends to happen in a three-step process.

First, we have a tendency, often unconsciously, to mimic the facial expressions of people we're with. When they smile, so do we. When they frown, we reflexively copy this too.

Next, we follow this mimicry by genuinely feeling the emotion it represents. I feel sad, I frown, you frown, you feel sad.

Finally, if people then share their experiences, their emotions become synchronized. When I tell you why I'm feeling low, you may also get low.

Sadness can be contagious, but fortunately so too can happiness. So if you feel a little below par, it may be worth spending time with positive people as some of their "upbeatness" could rub off on you. If you can, find a positive friend who tends to be a bit detached. They'll probably still be empathetic, but their detachment means there'll be less worry that you'll bring them down too.

Who do you know who's generally upbeat, but who keeps themselves a little detached?

....

How could you spend time in their company?
E.g. Suggest meeting for coffee, or going for a walk.

....

How can you get in touch with them, and when can you do this?

....

....

How to be around low moods without "catching" them.

Emotions can be more contagious than you might imagine. For instance, research has shown that if you and I are friends (and at this stage of our journey through the book, I hope we are) my moods will affect you. Not only that, though, my moods will affect your friends—who I probably don't know—

and, remarkably, even your friends' friends—who I almost certainly don't know. Emotions can spread through social networks like ripples on a pond.

Not surprisingly, you're likely to do best when surrounded with positive, upbeat people. But what if you can't be? What if there's someone in your life who tends to live at the bluer end of the mood spectrum?

There are two main strategies that can help.

The first is to distract yourself so that, as far as possible, this other person's moods aren't in your line of thought. Difficult, but possible.

The other is to "counter attack" with serenity and calmness. Again, tricky, but it can work.

We can't always choose who we spend our time with, but we do generally have a choice about how we react to them.

Is there someone in your life who tends to bring you down? Who?

....

Assuming you have no choice about being around them, which strategy might work best—distraction or "counter-attack"? Both?

....

When can you try this out?

....

....

16

One useful function of the book is the way it allows you to capture explanations in its "What happened?" boxes. When you look back, try to learn from them so you can avoid experiences that tend to lead to unhappiness.

How much are you experiencing these emotions and feelings right now?

Date: [   ]

	NOT AT ALL	VERY SLIGHTLY	A LITTLE	MODERATELY	QUITE A BIT	EXTREMELY
ANGRY	5	4	3	2	1	0
ANXIOUS	5	4	3	2	1	0
CHEERFUL	0	1	2	3	4	5
HEALTHY	0	1	2	3	4	5
IN PAIN	5	4	3	2	1	0
LONELY	5	4	3	2	1	0
LOVED	0	1	2	3	4	5
MOTIVATED	0	1	2	3	4	5
TIRED	5	4	3	2	1	0
UNDERSTOOD	0	1	2	3	4	5

Add numbers beside checked boxes — Total A: [   ]

Multiply Total A x 2. This is your Well-being Score out of 100: [   ]

Plot Well-being Score on graph on page 280, then

...What happened?

Finally, if your score is...
0-42   Turn to Nudge 16C
43-67   Turn to Nudge 16A
68-100   Turn to Nudge 16B

Make a three month plan.

Have there been times in your life when you felt as though you had little to look forward to? I've had them, and I know how distressing they were.

Setting goals and working towards them can help to give your life purpose and meaning, and things can seem hollow and meaningless when you don't have objectives.

Fortunately it's not impossible to solve the problem. How? Well you can start by making plans, always a little easier when you're not in the depths of despair.

My advice today is to think ahead, three months from now. Is there a birthday on the horizon? Is it going to be a holiday of some kind? Maybe something *could* happen around that time?

Okay, so now think about ways in which you, and perhaps others, might enjoy this more. Perhaps you could arrange, book, or schedule something now?

How does this sound?

Why not go ahead and set something up?

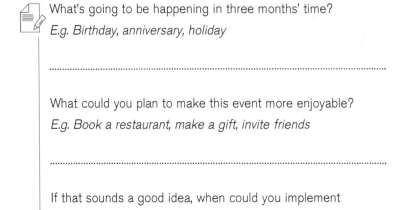

What's going to be happening in three months' time?
E.g. Birthday, anniversary, holiday

....

What could you plan to make this event more enjoyable?
E.g. Book a restaurant, make a gift, invite friends

....

If that sounds a good idea, when could you implement your plans?

....

Build on your strengths.

If we were to compile a top ten list of things happy people do differently, I suspect that setting themselves goals would be pretty near the top.

Giving yourself objectives is good. It builds optimism and delivers a sense of achievement and satisfaction when your goals are successfully accomplished. So since it seems you're in a fairly reasonable place today, maybe it's the right time to set yourself a goal or two?

Effective objectives need to be challenging enough to excite us, but they should also be achievable.

Perhaps I can make a suggestion, then. How would it feel to set yourself the goal of building up one of your strengths? Are you known for being kind? Or creative? Maybe others see you as persistent, or brave? While having strengths is great, developing them is even better.

How would it feel to be kinder, more creative, more persistent, or even braver in the next couple of months? Rather good I suspect.

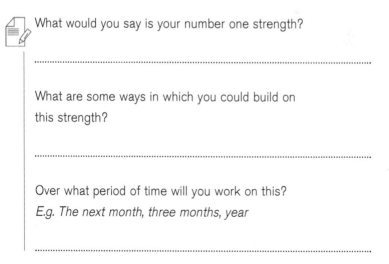

What would you say is your number one strength?

....

What are some ways in which you could build on this strength?

....

Over what period of time will you work on this?
E.g. The next month, three months, year

....

"I'd like to be a pessimist but I don't think I have it in me."

Right, with a line like that I don't have it in me to do stand-up comedy either.

Never mind. Joking aside, one side of pessimism that's definitely not funny is its tendency to strike when you already feel below par.

Optimism is likely to be in short supply on gloomy days.

But an ability to assume the best and have hope is an important builder of happiness. So how do you turn a stubborn, pessimistic outlook into a more positive, optimistic one?

Although it certainly helps to have things to look forward to, you're unlikely to set yourself ambitious goals on atrocious days. But that doesn't mean you can't set any at all, just that they need to be modest and achievable. It can also help to promise yourself a reward for meeting your objectives.

On a good day you can make big plans, but on a bad day simply getting up and showering can feel challenging enough. So keep your goals realistic. The big stuff can wait.

What modest goal can you set yourself for the day ahead?

....

When can you do this?

....

How will you reward yourself once it's done?

....

....

17

Try to ensure that you're somewhere comfortable when it's time to work with the book, as you'll concentrate better if you are.

How much are you experiencing these emotions and feelings right now?

Date: _____

	NOT AT ALL	VERY SLIGHTLY	A LITTLE	MODERATELY	QUITE A BIT	EXTREMELY
ANGRY	☐ 5	☐ 4	☐ 3	☐ 2	☐ 1	☐ 0
ANXIOUS	☐ 5	☐ 4	☐ 3	☐ 2	☐ 1	☐ 0
CHEERFUL	☐ 0	☐ 1	☐ 2	☐ 3	☐ 4	☐ 5
HEALTHY	☐ 0	☐ 1	☐ 2	☐ 3	☐ 4	☐ 5
IN PAIN	☐ 5	☐ 4	☐ 3	☐ 2	☐ 1	☐ 0
LONELY	☐ 5	☐ 4	☐ 3	☐ 2	☐ 1	☐ 0
LOVED	☐ 0	☐ 1	☐ 2	☐ 3	☐ 4	☐ 5
MOTIVATED	☐ 0	☐ 1	☐ 2	☐ 3	☐ 4	☐ 5
TIRED	☐ 5	☐ 4	☐ 3	☐ 2	☐ 1	☐ 0
UNDERSTOOD	☐ 0	☐ 1	☐ 2	☐ 3	☐ 4	☐ 5

Add numbers beside checked boxes – Total A: _____

Multiply Total A x 2. This is your Well-being Score out of 100: _____

Plot Well-being Score on graph on page 280, then

…What happened?

Finally, if your score is…
0-42   Turn to Nudge 17B
43-67   Turn to Nudge 17C
68-100   Turn to Nudge 17A

Reflect.

It's no accident that it takes a few minutes each day to complete the well-being questionnaires in this book.

As you know, rather than asking you to make a snap judgment about your well-being, the book asks you to rate yourself in ten dimensions.

Doing so should give you a more accurate score, but the very act of getting you to slow down and reflect is almost certainly doing you good in itself.

You see, we live in an accelerated world that allows us few opportunities to take stock of where we are in life.

We don't get many chances to celebrate our achievements either. As soon as one thing is finished, it's on to the next.

But celebration is a surprisingly effective way to boost well-being. It encourages us to appreciate the present rather than brood on the past, or fret about the future.

Right now I think you do have reason to celebrate, so I hope you will. Look back at your progress through the book and be pleased with today's score, which places you towards the top of the chart. Then mark your achievement in a way that makes most sense to you.

You're doing really well.

How do you feel about your progress through the book so far?

....

Would you agree that you have good cause to celebrate?

....

So how will you celebrate? When? How can I join you? (Just kidding.)

....

....

Celebrate a modest achievement.

GETTING
OUT OF
BED
AWARD

The original definition of the word "celebration" was honoring or praising publicly, and of course when we speak of a celebrated author we mean that he or she is a revered writer.

Over time, however, the word has evolved to primarily mean a social gathering or enjoyable activity that publicly acknowledges a significant or happy day or event.

I know, any excuse for a party. Speaking of which, I don't exactly count myself as being among the world's greatest party animals. Sad to say, although the odd party is okay, most of the time I'd rather stay at home with a good book.

Of course there's certainly one set of circumstances in which celebrating is distant from someone's mind, and that's when they feel a bit grim. However, although few would think of partying when their mood is low, this is in some respects a shame.

You see, taking time to recognize your achievements helps you focus on the positive and to feel grateful—both of which are happiness-builders. Even when you believe you've nothing to celebrate, there's nearly always something, even if it's an achievement as modest as getting out of bed and getting dressed, not easy on a tough day.

Over the course of the next 24 hours, why not look for an opportunity for the mini-est of mini celebrations: then reward yourself with a cup of coffee, a walk, your favorite TV show, or a soak in a hot bath?

Being realistic, what achievement could you celebrate today?

....

What will you do to celebrate it?

....

(Later.) So, how did that feel?

....

....

What was your success?

Nine months before the 1984 Olympics in Los Angeles, U.S. gymnast Bart Conner tore his bicep muscle. To be honest, it pretty much looked as if that would mark the end of his dreams, and he wouldn't make the Games. But not only did he fight his way back to full health, he took home two gold medals.

Later, when a television interviewer asked Conner how he had done it, he thanked his parents, explaining: "Every night before bed my parents would ask me what my success was. So I went to bed a success every night of my life. I woke up every morning a success. When I was injured before the Olympics, I knew I was going to make it back because I was a success every day of my life."

With parents like that, small wonder Bart Conner had such self-belief. But what about those of us who didn't grow up in such a nurturing environment?

Why don't we take a leaf out of Mr. and Mrs. Conner's book? Instead of being asked by someone else, let's put the question to ourselves. What was our success? Then celebrate it. Maybe not with a full-blown party, but definitely with a quiet sense of self-congratulation and pride.

What was your success in the past 24 hours?

....

Do you take pride in this? Why?

....

How does it make you feel to acknowledge and celebrate your success?

....

....

18

If possible, try to view your interactions with the book as positive and pleasant, rather than painful and punitive.
It's here to help, and wants to make the process as enjoyable as possible.

How much are you experiencing these emotions and feelings right now?

Date:

	NOT AT ALL	VERY SLIGHTLY	A LITTLE	MODERATELY	QUITE A BIT	EXTREMELY
ANGRY	5	4	3	2	1	0
ANXIOUS	5	4	3	2	1	0
CHEERFUL	0	1	2	3	4	5
HEALTHY	0	1	2	3	4	5
IN PAIN	5	4	3	2	1	0
LONELY	5	4	3	2	1	0
LOVED	0	1	2	3	4	5
MOTIVATED	0	1	2	3	4	5
TIRED	5	4	3	2	1	0
UNDERSTOOD	0	1	2	3	4	5

Add numbers beside checked boxes – Total A:

Multiply Total A x 2. This is your Well-being Score out of 100:

Plot Well-being Score on graph on page 280, then

...What happened?

Finally, if your score is...
0-42   Turn to Nudge 18B
43-67   Turn to Nudge 18A
68-100 Turn to Nudge 18C

Change your outfit, change your outlook.

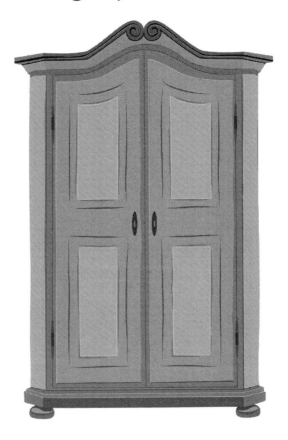

If you've dressed up for a job interview in the past, you'll probably know the effect your outfit can have on your mindset.

Formal clothes tend to give me gravitas and confidence. On the other hand, when I wear blue jeans and a T-shirt on weekends it helps me become more relaxed and laid back.

The sensation of feeling different because of what you're wearing starts within, and then gets amplified by other people's reactions. When I still lived in the U.K., I remember walking down the main street in Peterborough wearing—unusually for me—a business suit with a white shirt and tie. It may have been just my imagination, but I felt I could sense passers-by treating me with the tiniest bit of respect.

So could we apply this perception-warping effect for mood-boosting purposes?

Yes, I think so. Imagine what you'd wear on a day when you felt better about yourself, then dress in those clothes rather than whatever you might otherwise have worn. And stand by to feel better, if only a little.

Because every little counts.

What clothes would you wear on a happy day?

....

Could you wear them today, right now? Or soon?

....

When can you get changed?

....

....

Dress up.

In the musical *Bye Bye Birdie*, Albert Peterson (played by Dick Van Dyke) exhorts his secretary and sweetheart Rosie (Janet Leigh) to "put on a happy face." She doesn't, because when you feel low it's just not that easy.

Even though you'd assuredly love to feel better, you can't just slap on a sunnier disposition.

Or can you? I'm pretty sure there's a way to give yourself a happier appearance—by wearing clothes that give others the impression you're better than you actually are.

It's not uncommon for people to dress in baggy clothes and drab colors when they're low—it's a way of hiding. However, there's a school of thought that suggests dressing as though you feel good—shapely clothes in bright colors—can make a big difference.

But isn't doing this pulling a fast one? No, I don't think it is. To a certain extent others will treat you in a way that is prompted by your clothing.

So if you want to be seen as a depressed person, by all means wear over-sized, dull-colored clothes. But if you'd rather be treated more positively, why not put on something bright?

When people treat you positively, you're more likely to think positively. And when you think positively, you're more likely to feel good.

Do you normally wear big, dull clothes when you feel low?

....

What colors and styles do you wear when you feel more positive?

....

Is today a good one to make some style changes?

....

....

Lots of people believe they know what clothing colors suit their personalities, but I'm told that when clients engage image consultants they're often surprised by the colors they're advised to wear.

And just as there are colors that complement character, it's helpful to remember that what you wear can have a considerable impact on your mood.

Speaking of moods, since yours seems to be doing rather well at the moment, let's try keeping it that way, shall we?

Rather than dressing in drab colors today, put on the clothes of a happy person.

Lots of red can mean passion, but small red accents capture attention. Green is easy on the eye, and is connected with nature in our minds. Wear green when you need a mental refresh. Yellow is a psychologically strong color. Use it to boost your optimism and confidence.

Blue is calming and clear, associated with dependability and trustworthiness.

Black? It can give you power and professional presence.

To cut a long story short, wear clothes you know will make you feel good.

What colors and clothes do you choose when you want to feel good?

....

When can you next wear those colors?

....

(Later.) How did wearing your favorite colors make you feel?

....

....

19

You're likely to know where you want to go using this book, which is probably a place of greater happiness. But always remember that your journey may take the form of a series of small wins, rather than being one sudden sprint to the finish line.

How much are you experiencing these emotions and feelings right now?

Date: [   ]

	NOT AT ALL	VERY SLIGHTLY	A LITTLE	MODERATELY	QUITE A BIT	EXTREMELY
ANGRY	☐ 5	☐ 4	☐ 3	☐ 2	☐ 1	☐ 0
ANXIOUS	☐ 5	☐ 4	☐ 3	☐ 2	☐ 1	☐ 0
CHEERFUL	☐ 0	☐ 1	☐ 2	☐ 3	☐ 4	☐ 5
HEALTHY	☐ 0	☐ 1	☐ 2	☐ 3	☐ 4	☐ 5
IN PAIN	☐ 5	☐ 4	☐ 3	☐ 2	☐ 1	☐ 0
LONELY	☐ 5	☐ 4	☐ 3	☐ 2	☐ 1	☐ 0
LOVED	☐ 0	☐ 1	☐ 2	☐ 3	☐ 4	☐ 5
MOTIVATED	☐ 0	☐ 1	☐ 2	☐ 3	☐ 4	☐ 5
TIRED	☐ 5	☐ 4	☐ 3	☐ 2	☐ 1	☐ 0
UNDERSTOOD	☐ 0	☐ 1	☐ 2	☐ 3	☐ 4	☐ 5

Add numbers beside checked boxes – Total A: [   ]

Multiply Total A x 2. This is your Well-being Score out of 100: [   ]

Plot Well-being Score on graph on page 280, then

...What happened?

Finally, if your score is...
0-42   Turn to Nudge 19A
43-67   Turn to Nudge 19C
68-100 Turn to Nudge 19B

Are you thinking
in black and white?

It never rains but it pours, and sometimes the cards feel stacked against you, with one bad thing following another.

So how do you cope when you appear to have little control over what happens in your life? Well, while it's true that you sometimes can't change your circumstances, the one thing you can usually control is how you decide to think about them.

Of course it's not surprising that we feel negative emotions when bad stuff happens, and as a matter of fact it's genetically programmed into us. Our ancient ancestors depended on fear kicking in when a ferocious animal appeared out of the blue, for example. Being frightened helped them get the heck out of there, so the appropriately fearful survived, passing on their genes to us. The more laid-back tribe members? They got eaten.

Greatly limiting their ability to pass on *their* genes.

Fortunately the day-to-day world most of us now occupy features few scary animals, but evolution is slow. Our brains haven't necessarily changed that much.

Actively encouraging yourself to think positive thoughts is therefore important.

One way to do this is to avoid "black and white" thinking. You may tell yourself that life is awful—a black view. A white view is that life is fantastic. But in reality neither of these is probably true. The answer is more likely to be some shade of gray between the two extremes.

Maybe thinking in this way will help you today.

What example of black and white thinking might you be doing?

E.g. My personal life is a disaster

....

What would be the complete opposite of this?

E.g. My personal life is blissfully happy

....

....

What is the more likely "shade of gray" truth?

E.g. My personal life could be better, but it's not all bad

....

....

Don't take things personally.

I think few would disagree with the general principle that if you want to be happy it helps to have more positive thoughts than negative ones. However, in 2011 a paper appeared in a respected scientific journal suggesting that in order to flourish, any one person should experience precisely 2.9013 times as many positive emotions as negative ones.

Now if this sounds suspiciously exact to you, you'd be quite right to raise your eyebrows. In fact, the mathematics behind the paper was subsequently decisively debunked by a rookie psychologist who described the ratio as a "brain fart".

Quite. However I don't think we should let a quibble over math prevent us from accepting that, even if it can't be pinned down to 4 decimal places, there's probably something in the idea of having more positive thoughts than negatives.

So how do you encourage even more positive thoughts than you may be experiencing right now? One way is to avoid a type of "thinking error" called personalization, where you tell yourself that anything that goes wrong is your fault. For instance, if someone was rude to you while you were driving, the personalization-thinking interpretation might be "I did something wrong". But the truth could easily be that the other person was simply having a rough day.

Try to think more positive thoughts than negative ones today, even if it can't be exactly 2.9013 times as many.

Are you currently seeing an issue in a very personalized way?
E.g. Someone at work dislikes me because she thinks I'm stupid

....

Is there a less personalized way to view this? What is it?
E.g. Actually she thinks everyone is stupid, and that's her problem—not mine.

....

....

You can only think one thought at a time.

What's your favorite food? I'll give you a moment.

Okay, if you just mentally answered me you'll have shown yourself that our brains are actually pretty adept at answering our questions.

Sometimes this can be advantageous, but not always. An

example of when it's not so helpful? Imagine you were having one of those average kinds of day, but kept asking yourself "Shouldn't there be more to life than this?" Now while there's no harm in a little self-reflection every now and then, it's not really helpful to get yourself into one of these self-defeating spirals of dissatisfaction.

So if you'd like to change a somewhat negative mindset into a more positive one, take advantage of your brain's capacity to have no more than one thought at a time.

An example could be to ask yourself "When in my life have I been really lucky?" One way or another, most of us have had a certain amount of luck. Recalling positive times from the past can help you feel more positive about the present.

Is there a negative question you're asking yourself right now?
E.g. Why is my job so awful? Why do I hate the way I look?

....

Can you think of a more positive question to replace it?
E.g. What have I done in the past that's worth remembering? Who have been my best friends in life?

....

How will you remind yourself to replace the negative question with the positive?
E.g. Write myself a reminder and leave it where I'll see it.

....

....

20

No matter how young or old you are, you're bound to have accumulated wisdom and experience as your life has unfolded, and now it's time to comb the recesses of your memory as you recall how you coped with emotional health challenges in the past.

How much are you experiencing these emotions and feelings right now?

Date: _____

	NOT AT ALL	VERY SLIGHTLY	A LITTLE	MODERATELY	QUITE A BIT	EXTREMELY
ANGRY	☐ 5	☐ 4	☐ 3	☐ 2	☐ 1	☐ 0
ANXIOUS	☐ 5	☐ 4	☐ 3	☐ 2	☐ 1	☐ 0
CHEERFUL	☐ 0	☐ 1	☐ 2	☐ 3	☐ 4	☐ 5
HEALTHY	☐ 0	☐ 1	☐ 2	☐ 3	☐ 4	☐ 5
IN PAIN	☐ 5	☐ 4	☐ 3	☐ 2	☐ 1	☐ 0
LONELY	☐ 5	☐ 4	☐ 3	☐ 2	☐ 1	☐ 0
LOVED	☐ 0	☐ 1	☐ 2	☐ 3	☐ 4	☐ 5
MOTIVATED	☐ 0	☐ 1	☐ 2	☐ 3	☐ 4	☐ 5
TIRED	☐ 5	☐ 4	☐ 3	☐ 2	☐ 1	☐ 0
UNDERSTOOD	☐ 0	☐ 1	☐ 2	☐ 3	☐ 4	☐ 5

Add numbers beside checked boxes – Total A: _____

Multiply Total A x 2. This is your Well-being Score out of 100: _____

Plot Well-being Score on graph on page 280, then

...What happened?

Finally, if your score is...
0-42   Turn to Nudge 20A
43-67   Turn to Nudge 20C
68-100   Turn to Nudge 20B

Funny old thing, laughter.

During get-togethers after funerals it's not uncommon to hear laughter.

Does this imply disrespect for the person who passed away?

No. Mirth at a time like this is actually a perfectly normal human reaction.

It defuses the distress and discomfort people are likely to have felt leading up to the event, and in any case, it's also true that we're more likely to laugh when we're in the company of others.

So can knowing we have the capacity to laugh in sad situations help when we're in a low mood? Yes.

Invite an audience of sad people into a cinema showing a comedy, and you'll almost certainly hear the odd giggle.

Why not use this to your own advantage if life is dealing you a poor hand?

Laughter can be good for you, and while a brief chuckle isn't going to make you instantly happy, it can certainly make you instantaneously happier.

The effects can last too.

On a bad day it can help to watch comedy clips on YouTube. If you can't immediately think of one, search for "laughing baby." That always works for me.

What's guaranteed to make you laugh?
E.g. A clip from a comedy, a favorite book

....

When can you schedule five minutes with this?

....

(Later.) Did you laugh? How did that make you feel?

....

....

Chuckle yourself cheerful.

Gelotology sounds science-y, and is. It also feels like it could be something to do with ice cream, but isn't. No, gelotology is the study of laughter and its physiological and psychological effects on the body.

Actually, although most people accept we often feel better

after a good laugh, scientists say they can't be sure why, exactly. But maybe this doesn't matter. It certainly didn't to newspaper editor Norman Cousins (no relation) who in 1979 wrote the book *Anatomy of an Illness*, about his remarkable self-management of a painful spine condition.

Discharging himself from hospital, he took a borrowed film projector into a hotel room to watch night after night of Marx Bros movies and episodes of *Candid Camera*. Amazingly, every twenty minutes of laughter gave him two hours free from pain.

But perhaps we shouldn't be surprised, because laughter relaxes us. It boosts your immune system and triggers the release of endorphins (probably what helped alleviate Norman Cousins's chronic pain). It may protect your heart. And of course laughter is also great at bringing people closer together.

Since you're already feeling good, laughter may come more easily to you. Why not look for laughter opportunities today?

What or who has a tendency to make you laugh?

....

Can you plan to get more of that in the next day? How?
E.g. Watch a favorite comedy, arrange a call with that friend who has the great sense of humor

....

When will you do this?

....

....

Who makes you laugh?

The psychologist Robert Provine of the University of Maryland wrote the book on laughter. Literally. He's the author of *Laughter: A Scientific Investigation*.

Professor Provine says that although laughter may make us healthier, we don't really know why. Fair enough, really. Since

I'm sure neither of us doubts that laughing feels good, maybe we don't need to understand the underlying science. On the other hand, one thing Robert Provine is certain about is that we're much more likely to laugh when we're in the company of other people. Thirty times more likely, in fact.

And of course laughter is a terrific way to strengthen relationships. It's a kind of social glue.

What does this mean to you on a day that might be described as "fair to middling"?

It may be a good prompt for you to seek the company of someone who makes you laugh: I'm sure you know who they are. Even better if this person is someone who laughs back with gusto when you laugh.

Is laughter the best medicine? Well it's pretty good, although if you're headed for surgery I'd opt for a general anesthetic as well. Just to be on the safe side.

Who do you know that's just about guaranteed to make you chuckle?

....

How could you get together? (Laughter works better face-to-face or on the phone than it does by text.)

....

When will you get together? Soon is good.

....

....

21

Today marks three weeks that you've been using the book, and that means there are just nine days left. Hopefully you've experienced at least a certain amount of progress. What's next? Just keep going.

How much are you experiencing these emotions and feelings right now?

Date:

	NOT AT ALL	VERY SLIGHTLY	A LITTLE	MODERATELY	QUITE A BIT	EXTREMELY
ANGRY	5	4	3	2	1	0
ANXIOUS	5	4	3	2	1	0
CHEERFUL	0	1	2	3	4	5
HEALTHY	0	1	2	3	4	5
IN PAIN	5	4	3	2	1	0
LONELY	5	4	3	2	1	0
LOVED	0	1	2	3	4	5
MOTIVATED	0	1	2	3	4	5
TIRED	5	4	3	2	1	0
UNDERSTOOD	0	1	2	3	4	5

Add numbers beside checked boxes – Total A:

Multiply Total A x 2. This is your Well-being Score out of 100:

Plot Well-being Score on graph on page 280, then

...What happened?

Finally, if your score is...
0-42   Turn to Nudge 21B
43-67   Turn to Nudge 21C
68-100   Turn to Nudge 21A

A little silliness never hurt anyone.

Bronnie Ware, an Australian nurse who spent several years caring for patients in their final three months of life, was in a sad but ideal position to learn more about people's regrets.

In fact she went on to write the book *The Top Five Regrets of the Dying.*

Close to the top of the list was "I wish that I had let myself be happier." As Bronnie Ware said: "Fear of change had them pretending to others, and to their selves, that they were content. When deep within, they longed to laugh properly and have silliness in their life again."

I hope you and I have more than three months left, in which case we have an opportunity to minimize the chance that we will one day regret not letting ourselves be happier.

You're probably doing quite well today, so it's a great time to make plans, and perhaps you already have. Don't only make serious ones, though.

Leave room in your schedule for happiness, and when it shows up at your door, welcome it in with open arms.

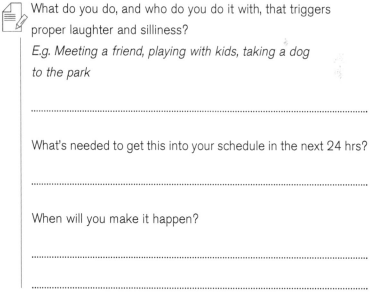

What do you do, and who do you do it with, that triggers proper laughter and silliness?

E.g. Meeting a friend, playing with kids, taking a dog to the park

What's needed to get this into your schedule in the next 24 hrs?

When will you make it happen?

Leave space for happiness.

RESERVED

Full-time workers diagnosed with depression are likely to be absent for around nine working days a year because of health problems, around five days more than workers with no depression, according to figures from Gallup in the U.S.A.

This probably won't come as a surprise, and in fact I've had more than my fair share of days in the past when a low mood made it hard to work.

If anything, it's maybe more surprising that people suffering from serious depression make it to the office at all on the other 240 working days of the year.

The thing is, though, even when you feel low you probably manage to stick to at least a few routines and schedules. And that's no mean achievement.

Knowing this, I wonder if you've ever considered scheduling "happiness opportunities"? I know it sounds a bit weird but happiness isn't necessarily just going to show up at your doorstep like the mail delivery.

I'm guessing you'd like to be happier, and I'm fairly sure happiness would be pretty high on your Wanted list. Maybe, therefore, it should also be on your To-Do list?

What things made you a little happier on gray days in the past? *E.g. Walk in the park, reading favorite book, playing with a kid*

....

Which of these could you do today?

....

When can you put this on your schedule?

....

....

Schedule the things that make you happy.

Stanford University professor Jennifer Aaker makes a simple but profound point when she says: "It's really that simple: the things that make you happy, do them more often." Which when you think about it is wise advice, that many of us don't take.

For most of my life happiness has only ever turned up like an uninvited, albeit welcome, guest at a party.

The thing is though, life gets busy. There are things to do, places to be, people to meet. And if we're not careful, we become so busy being busy that we fail to grasp opportunities to follow Jennifer Aaker's wise advice.

So how do we tackle this? Fortunately it's fairly easy.

If happiness is important to you, make it an important part of your schedule.

Quite simply, plan times to do the things that make you happy, and when you do so, don't pencil them in. Ink them in. They're that important.

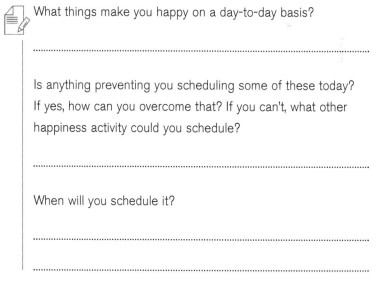

What things make you happy on a day-to-day basis?

....

Is anything preventing you scheduling some of these today? If yes, how can you overcome that? If you can't, what other happiness activity could you schedule?

....

When will you schedule it?

....

....

22

Most people will probably spend around an hour a week with this book, which is about the length of a psychotherapy session. What's more, the book is here whenever you need it.

How much are you experiencing these emotions and feelings right now?

Date: [   ]

	NOT AT ALL	VERY SLIGHTLY	A LITTLE	MODERATELY	QUITE A BIT	EXTREMELY
ANGRY	☐ 5	☐ 4	☐ 3	☐ 2	☐ 1	☐ 0
ANXIOUS	☐ 5	☐ 4	☐ 3	☐ 2	☐ 1	☐ 0
CHEERFUL	☐ 0	☐ 1	☐ 2	☐ 3	☐ 4	☐ 5
HEALTHY	☐ 0	☐ 1	☐ 2	☐ 3	☐ 4	☐ 5
IN PAIN	☐ 5	☐ 4	☐ 3	☐ 2	☐ 1	☐ 0
LONELY	☐ 5	☐ 4	☐ 3	☐ 2	☐ 1	☐ 0
LOVED	☐ 0	☐ 1	☐ 2	☐ 3	☐ 4	☐ 5
MOTIVATED	☐ 0	☐ 1	☐ 2	☐ 3	☐ 4	☐ 5
TIRED	☐ 5	☐ 4	☐ 3	☐ 2	☐ 1	☐ 0
UNDERSTOOD	☐ 0	☐ 1	☐ 2	☐ 3	☐ 4	☐ 5

Add numbers beside checked boxes – Total A: [   ]

Multiply Total A x 2. This is your Well-being Score out of 100: [   ]

Plot Well-being Score on graph on page 280, then

...What happened?

Finally, if your score is...
0-42   Turn to Nudge 22B
43-67   Turn to Nudge 22C
68-100 Turn to Nudge 22A

Catch yourself doing something right.

Being comfortable with who you are is easier when you feel good, as you seem to be right now.

Despite this, however, when we stop to evaluate ourselves it could be our faults and weaknesses that come to mind rather than our strengths.

When Ken Blanchard and Spencer Johnson wrote *The One Minute Manager* in 1982 they discouraged managers from finding fault with their staff, suggesting they should instead "catch people doing things right," praising them for one minute.

Blanchard and Johnson were great believers in short and sweet interactions.

I wonder if that idea might inspire you to action?

As you go about your day, why not look out for things you do pretty well?

Catch yourself doing things right and at least inwardly give yourself the credit you're due.

What are three things you do well in your day-to-day life?

1. ....

2. ....

3. ....

What makes these skills or behaviors impressive?

....

How might someone else praise you for them?

....

....

Love you.

I'm no saint, but since one of my underlying values in life is kindness, I'm ashamed to admit I can't claim a flawless record in this regard.

I must confess that one person in particular has suffered

from a lack of consideration from me that borders on the down-right cruel. They've had it far worse from me than anyone else who's been in my life.

So who is this poor beleaguered individual? Why, me of course. Over the years I think I've been too tough on myself, too thoughtless.

But you know what? I'm pretty sure I'm not alone. Maybe you also feel you've been unforgiving and mean to yourself? Of course, when you go through a difficult patch it's pretty common to dislike yourself to some degree.

So is this you? I'm sorry of course, but I have to say you're not alone. The kindest thing you can do is treat yourself as you would a good friend. Would you tell them they were useless and a failure? Would you offer them no hope, no encouragement?

I think not.

You may not be perfect (who is?) but you're you, and to be comfortable with this is such an important step to take.

What's an example of something you tell yourself that you'd never tell a friend?

....

What *would* you say to a friend in similar circumstances?

....

What will you therefore say to yourself?

....

....

Be comfortable with who you are.

The British author Charles Handy suggests that as people age they become more comfortable with who they are.

He says: "Bald or old or fat or poor, successful or struggling—when you don't feel the need to apologize for anything or to deny anything. To be comfortable in your own skin is the beginning of strength."

Accepting yourself for who you are is an important foundation of happiness, but self-acceptance isn't always easy in a world that seems to demand "better, faster, stronger".

Kristin Neff, a leading psychologist, says an important principle of self-acceptance is recognizing that you're not the only one to mess up or have faults.

Doing so will give you a sense of connection to others which then enables you to show the same compassion for yourself as you do for others.

Maybe you have doubts about yourself?

It wouldn't be surprising, nearly everyone does. But how would you reassure someone else with similar thoughts?

Perhaps you doubt something about yourself at the moment? What?

....

What might you say or do to reassure someone with similar concerns?

....

How can you "give this message to yourself"?
E.g. Write myself a note, make a collage

....

....

23

Perhaps you can view the line of your graph as a piece of thread connecting your days. Does it do so in a tightly controlled way, or does it wander erratically? Look for patterns, learn your ways.

How much are you experiencing these emotions and feelings right now?

Date: _____

	NOT AT ALL	VERY SLIGHTLY	A LITTLE	MODERATELY	QUITE A BIT	EXTREMELY
ANGRY	☐ 5	☐ 4	☐ 3	☐ 2	☐ 1	☐ 0
ANXIOUS	☐ 5	☐ 4	☐ 3	☐ 2	☐ 1	☐ 0
CHEERFUL	☐ 0	☐ 1	☐ 2	☐ 3	☐ 4	☐ 5
HEALTHY	☐ 0	☐ 1	☐ 2	☐ 3	☐ 4	☐ 5
IN PAIN	☐ 5	☐ 4	☐ 3	☐ 2	☐ 1	☐ 0
LONELY	☐ 5	☐ 4	☐ 3	☐ 2	☐ 1	☐ 0
LOVED	☐ 0	☐ 1	☐ 2	☐ 3	☐ 4	☐ 5
MOTIVATED	☐ 0	☐ 1	☐ 2	☐ 3	☐ 4	☐ 5
TIRED	☐ 5	☐ 4	☐ 3	☐ 2	☐ 1	☐ 0
UNDERSTOOD	☐ 0	☐ 1	☐ 2	☐ 3	☐ 4	☐ 5

Add numbers beside checked boxes − Total A: _____

Multiply Total A x 2. This is your Well-being Score out of 100: _____

Plot Well-being Score on graph on page 280, then

...What happened?

Finally, if your score is...
0-42   Turn to Nudge 23B
43-67   Turn to Nudge 23C
68-100 Turn to Nudge 23A

Does your life have meaning?

We always knew every September would be good for business when I ran an ad agency in London.

With the summer over, our clients returned to work with renewed focus, knowing there was a lot to be done before Christmas.

It always felt as if there was energy and drive to spare in September. Plans were hatched, progress was made.

I think in life, as in business, that it's easier to ask the big questions when things are good, which they may be for you right now. So perhaps this is an appropriate time to ask yourself what you see as your purpose and mission in life?

We all do better when we feel part of something bigger, so I wonder how this applies to you?

Do you feel you're using your unique strengths in a way that makes the most of them?

To some, living a life of meaning can materialize by being a follower of a religion.

For others it may emerge through the work we do, the family we're part of, or the friends we love. Today may be a good day to try answering the difficult questions.

What gives your life meaning?
E.g. Religious faith, the work I do, my family, or friends

....

What could give it even more meaning?
E.g. Spiritual study, more socially-minded work,
more time with family/friends

....

What small first step could you make towards this right now?

....

....

NUDGE 23B

In the next five minutes the world's population will have increased by no less than 1,250, which is more than the total number of students in my secondary (high) school.

In round numbers there are seven billion people on the planet, a colossal number, so each of us really ought to feel part of something way bigger than ourselves.

However the truth is that when you go through a rough patch it's pretty normal to feel as if it's you against the rest of the world. 6,999,999,999 to one.

And this is tough and unhelpful because feeling part of something bigger can be a remarkably valuable builder of happiness and well-being.

So is there some kind of quick fix for bad days? Well yes, I think there is, at least to a certain extent.

Today it may help to remember that your life does indeed have meaning, and that you do indeed have a purpose.

Small actions can help.

In some ways we're not seven billion individuals, but part of a gigantic machine, so why not remind yourself of this by making modest but meaningful contributions?

Perhaps you could offer to help someone carry an awkward load. You might pick up a couple of pieces of litter in the street. Or maybe you'll help calm an anxious pet left outside a store.

Why not look for tiny chances today to help you feel part of this amazing organism we call humankind?

How much do you currently feel part of something bigger?

....

If your answer's "not much", what could you do to fix this just a little today?
E.g. Look for chances to help others

....

(Later.) How did it feel to do this?

....

....

The mayfly's entire life is just one day.

Make the most of yours.

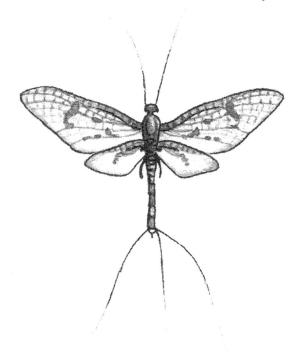

Imagine being a mayfly. If you wanted to make the most of your life, you'd need to pack a great deal into a short time. Although there are around 2,500 species of mayflies, none has a lifespan longer than a couple of days.

Some last only a few hours.

Now I think it's safe to assume that no mayflies will be reading this book. Quite right too. With such short lives I hope they've better things to do with their time.

I hope you and I have longer to live than a mayfly, and we'll rightly want our days on earth to be rewarding, healthy and happy. One way to make this more feasible is to help your life have as much meaning and purpose as possible.

If it already does, great. But if you sometimes feel you'd like to be part of something bigger, a useful exercise can be to imagine you only have, say, two years of life left.

What would you do to make a difference, to leave some kind of legacy? Could you use your strengths to leave the world a better place? A little reflection like this can go a long way. Especially when you remember that two years is 730 times longer than the average mayfly lives.

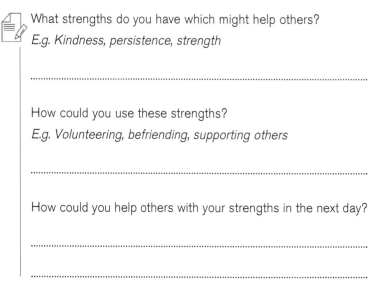

What strengths do you have which might help others?
E.g. Kindness, persistence, strength

....

How could you use these strengths?
E.g. Volunteering, befriending, supporting others

....

How could you help others with your strengths in the next day?

....

....

24

Although some choose to use this book completely privately, others find it helpful to discuss their progress with someone close to them, perhaps by sharing their graph. What do you think? If you're not already doing so, could this work for you?

How much are you experiencing these emotions and feelings right now?

Date: [   ]

	NOT AT ALL	VERY SLIGHTLY	A LITTLE	MODERATELY	QUITE A BIT	EXTREMELY
ANGRY	5	4	3	2	1	0
ANXIOUS	5	4	3	2	1	0
CHEERFUL	0	1	2	3	4	5
HEALTHY	0	1	2	3	4	5
IN PAIN	5	4	3	2	1	0
LONELY	5	4	3	2	1	0
LOVED	0	1	2	3	4	5
MOTIVATED	0	1	2	3	4	5
TIRED	5	4	3	2	1	0
UNDERSTOOD	0	1	2	3	4	5

Add numbers beside checked boxes – Total A: [   ]

Multiply Total A x 2. This is your Well-being Score out of 100: [   ]

Plot Well-being Score on graph on page 280, then

...What happened?

Finally, if your score is...
0-42   Turn to Nudge 24A
43-67   Turn to Nudge 24C
68-100 Turn to Nudge 24B

"How are you sleeping?"

It's a question often asked by doctors when they're interested in the emotional health of patients. People who aren't doing so well often either sleep too little or too much, but however you are at the moment there's no denying how satisfying it can be to get a full night's sleep.

I'm guessing many of us would love to sleep deeper or longer, so it could be useful to know that a proven way to get better nights is to spend fifteen minutes before you shut your eyes making a list of a few things you have to be thankful for in a gratitude journal.

If you like, keep a notebook and pen beside your bed to make this easier. It's an easy process that can be tremendously calming.

While it's maybe not bedtime yet, why not experience the effect of counting your blessings right now? Then do so again at the end of the day.

 Take a few minutes to list five things you're grateful for:

1. ....

2. ....

3. ....

4. ....

5. ....

How did it feel to do this?

....

....

According to research by Robert Emmons, a leading expert in the field of gratitude, saying thank you can deliver big psychological benefits. Grateful people tend to be happier and experience depression less.

Although we probably don't always remember to express gratitude, it's relatively easy to be thankful for good things.

Of course, it's harder to be grateful for negative experiences. How could you ever thank the person who fires you from your job, for example? Bear with me on this one, though, because gratitude in that kind of situation can be hugely rewarding, and it can also help speed up your recovery.

Let's consider the example of being fired. Almost certainly, the person who's "letting you go" isn't doing so for spiteful or vindictive reasons: it's fairly sure to be a business decision, and firing people is hands-down the worst part of being a manager.

He or she probably didn't sleep a wink the night before talking to you, and felt sick having to go through with it.

Empathizing with them can give you a genuine reason to say: "Thank you for being brave and professional enough to go through with this." You'll probably feel hurt, shocked, and devastated of course—a real smorgasbord of negative emotion.

However, being strong enough to thank your "executioner" will boost your self-respect while also reminding yourself not to take it too personally.

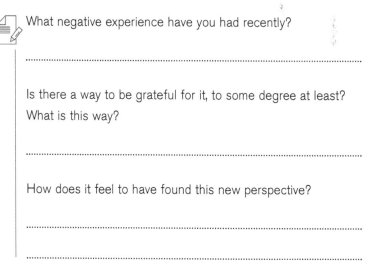

What negative experience have you had recently?

....

Is there a way to be grateful for it, to some degree at least? What is this way?

....

How does it feel to have found this new perspective?

....

....

I'm always warmed to see most people thanking the bus driver as they step off the shuttle between Palo Alto railway station and the Stanford University campus. Call me old-fashioned, but I think manners go a heck of a way. The great majority of passengers say one of three things: Thanks, Thank you, or Thank you very much.

Just recently though, someone shook things up in a way I'm sure the driver found heartening. What did this gentleman say to make such an impact?

Quite simply he added some specifics to his gratitude. "Thanks for getting me to work on time every morning." Nice. He even looked the driver in the eye as he said it.

Expressing gratitude is good for the person being thanked, and great for the person doing the thanking. In fact grateful people tend to be happier and less depressed.

However, the happiest and least depressed are those who are habitually specific.

So don't just thank someone, explain why you're thanking them, in as much detail as possible.

Who could you thank today?

....

What specifics could you add to your thanks?

....

When are you going to express your gratitude?

....

....

25

Recovering from a low mood is usually a slow and steady process. So when this happens, be kind to yourself. Don't always assume you'll see overnight success.

How much are you experiencing these emotions and feelings right now?

Date: [   ]

	NOT AT ALL	VERY SLIGHTLY	A LITTLE	MODERATELY	QUITE A BIT	EXTREMELY
ANGRY	☐ 5	☐ 4	☐ 3	☐ 2	☐ 1	☐ 0
ANXIOUS	☐ 5	☐ 4	☐ 3	☐ 2	☐ 1	☐ 0
CHEERFUL	☐ 0	☐ 1	☐ 2	☐ 3	☐ 4	☐ 5
HEALTHY	☐ 0	☐ 1	☐ 2	☐ 3	☐ 4	☐ 5
IN PAIN	☐ 5	☐ 4	☐ 3	☐ 2	☐ 1	☐ 0
LONELY	☐ 5	☐ 4	☐ 3	☐ 2	☐ 1	☐ 0
LOVED	☐ 0	☐ 1	☐ 2	☐ 3	☐ 4	☐ 5
MOTIVATED	☐ 0	☐ 1	☐ 2	☐ 3	☐ 4	☐ 5
TIRED	☐ 5	☐ 4	☐ 3	☐ 2	☐ 1	☐ 0
UNDERSTOOD	☐ 0	☐ 1	☐ 2	☐ 3	☐ 4	☐ 5

Add numbers beside checked boxes – Total A: [   ]

Multiply Total A x 2. This is your Well-being Score out of 100: [   ]

Plot Well-being Score on graph on page 280, then

...What happened?

Finally, if your score is...
0-42   Turn to Nudge 25A
43-67   Turn to Nudge 25B
68-100 Turn to Nudge 25C

Tickle your mood buds.

Imagine being in the shoes of my friend Josh and I when we ate at a restaurant in Beijing a few years ago. Understanding barely any Chinese made things tricky in an establishment whose waiters spoke no English, and whose menus offered no translations.

But being hungry and determined to order, we looked at the grilled fish that had been ordered by a neighboring table and attempted to convince our waiter with ludicrous sign-language that we'd like the same.

It wasn't that easy though. It never is. Opening up part of the menu that may or may not have been devoted to the type of fish we'd indicated, he appeared to wish us to select a version of it. We pointed randomly, at which he raised his eyebrows, shrugged, and set off for the kitchen.

When our order arrived, it was outrageously spicy. Apparently we'd inadvertently chosen the vindaloo equivalent. With tears in our eyes—well, in mine at least—Josh and I bravely demolished the whole dish.

We laughed about it afterwards, but if you want a rewarding dining experience it can help if you understand the menu and know what you'll probably enjoy.

In the same way, when you feel under the weather it makes sense to know what things make you happy. Then you can set out to do more of them.

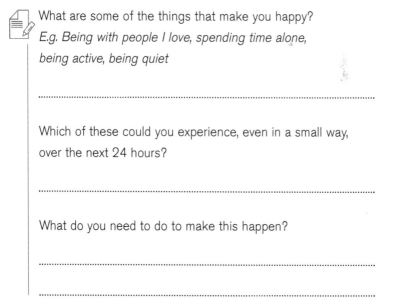

What are some of the things that make you happy?
E.g. Being with people I love, spending time alone, being active, being quiet

....

Which of these could you experience, even in a small way, over the next 24 hours?

....

What do you need to do to make this happen?

....

....

Which way's happiness?

When Alice in Wonderland met the Cheshire Cat sitting in the bough of a tree, she asked it which way she should go.

"That depends a good deal on where you want to get to," replied the cat, to which Alice said she didn't much care.

"Then," said the cat, "it doesn't matter which way you go."

Sadly it's easy at times to drift through life with little real thought about where you're headed. Easy but not uncommon— you wouldn't be the first to have realized you have a general lack of direction.

Perhaps I may offer a suggestion though? I guess many of us might place happiness pretty high on a list of where we'd like to be. But wanting happiness without knowing what makes us happy is not that different from being in Alice's situation.

It may help today if you think about what makes you happy, listening to your body as you do so.

Does it tense up and feel troubled or heavy as you reflect on certain parts of your life? Does it feel lighter and unfettered when you focus on other aspects?

What makes you happy? Listen to your body when you ask yourself this.

....

How much of that is currently in your life?

....

How can you get more of it?

....

....

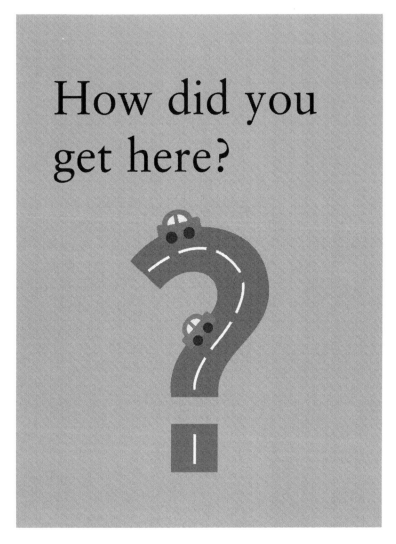

How did you get here?

Have you ever reached your destination after driving a familiar route only to realize that you can't remember a thing about the journey?

Actually it's a commonplace phenomenon known to psychologists as "driving without awareness."

(I really hope it didn't take someone too long to come up with such an imaginative label.)

Anyway, this type of driving is most likely done on a monotonous journey you've made many times before. It makes me wonder if you and I might occasionally be guilty of what one might call "living without awareness"?

When life becomes routine and uneventful, perhaps we drift along without giving it much attention.

So, although you may be doing well at the moment, it might be that you don't really know how you got here.

Let's definitely not knock feeling good, please, but at the same time perhaps it could be helpful to give due attention to the things that make you happy. Do you know what they are? How likely are you to mindfully schedule the kinds of activities and meetings that have made you happy in the past?

Today may be a good time to do exactly that.

Can you list three things (or people) that have made you happy in the past?

....

....

....

Would you like to experience more of these/them?

....

When can you do so?

....

26

When you record bad experiences, does it set them in stone? That's one way to look at it, but another (better) way is to regard them as having been moved from mind to paper so you no longer have to dwell on them.

How much are you experiencing these emotions and feelings right now?

Date: [   ]

	NOT AT ALL	VERY SLIGHTLY	A LITTLE	MODERATELY	QUITE A BIT	EXTREMELY
ANGRY	5	4	3	2	1	0
ANXIOUS	5	4	3	2	1	0
CHEERFUL	0	1	2	3	4	5
HEALTHY	0	1	2	3	4	5
IN PAIN	5	4	3	2	1	0
LONELY	5	4	3	2	1	0
LOVED	0	1	2	3	4	5
MOTIVATED	0	1	2	3	4	5
TIRED	5	4	3	2	1	0
UNDERSTOOD	0	1	2	3	4	5

Add numbers beside checked boxes – Total A: [   ]

Multiply Total A x 2. This is your Well-being Score out of 100: [   ]

Plot Well-being Score on graph on page 280, then

...What happened?

Finally, if your score is...
0-42   Turn to Nudge 26C
43-67   Turn to Nudge 26A
68-100   Turn to Nudge 26B

Hey, you with the billionaire's wealth.

As I write this, *Forbes* magazine tells me Bill Gates is the world's richest person, as he has been for 16 of the past 21 years. His net worth is a whopping $79.2 billion, yet there's one asset of which you and he have precisely the same amount. Yes, you and William Henry Gates III both have precisely 86,400 seconds per day. No more, no less.

Okay, I'm sure Mr. Gates has support staff to help him manage his 86,400 seconds (most of them, anyway—even multi-billionaires must have to do what multi-billionaires have to do) but I think we can safely conclude that he must be a pretty focused and organized kind of guy.

Do you find your own schedule getting over-full and over-complicated at times? I know I do. In an increasingly complex world, there's a lot to be said for simplicity, and this applies to time just as much as it does to a de-cluttered home or office.

So whenever you feel there are too many demands on your time, just stop. Ask yourself what's important and what isn't. Focus on your priorities instead of everyone else's. And don't forget to include time for rest, and time with loved ones.

Are there times in your week that are over-complex, over-scheduled? What are these times?

....

What are you doing during these demanding times that isn't really important?

....

What could you do today to simplify your schedule?

....

....

Don Norman, the director of the design lab at the University of California, San Diego, is a proponent of keeping things simple and usable.

He tells, however, of visiting a department store in South Korea where he noticed that the washing machines made domestically were all far more complicated than their imported counterparts. He asked his guides why.

"Because Koreans like things to look complex," they replied.

And I guess they had a point.

Haven't we all compared two similar products and picked the one with the most features?

The thing is however, complexity can get too much, and in fact, there seems to be a clear connection between simplicity and happiness.

As you appear to be doing pretty well at the moment, it may be that you have no unwanted complexity in your life.

However I suspect that just like most people, things could be simpler.

Since you feel good, therefore, now may be a suitable time to rid yourself of unneeded complications.

Do this one piece at a time, though.

Don't overwhelm yourself with sudden change.

Is there an area of your life that's more complicated than you'd like it to be?

....

How might this be simplified?

....

How could you start this process in the next 24 hours?

....

....

Keep
things
simple.

When we complain that someone can't see the forest for the trees, we're suggesting they're over-focused on detail to the extent that they cannot see the big picture.

I think this happens inadvertently when you feel low. It's easy to become distracted by the things, people and events immediately surrounding you, especially if they're complicated. And complexity can leave you feeling worse rather than better.

One tactic for rough times, therefore, could be to take active steps to simplify your day-to-day life.

A simple example?

When I've felt low in the past, I've been inclined to allow my dirty dishes to mount up in the kitchen. The higher the stack, the worse it felt.

A straightforward answer was to use the same plates, mug, and tableware for each meal, washing and drying them immediately after eating.

It kept the sink clear, and meant the utensils were ready and waiting for their next use.

Simplifying your life probably won't lead to overnight bliss, but it might at least be a step on the journey towards that light at the end of the tunnel.

Which areas of life currently feel complicated to you?

....

What could you do to simplify them? Small first steps are fine.

....

When will you do this?

....

....

27

By now you may have identified that certain activities, or people, aren't great for you emotionally. So if you find yourself doing something or being around someone that drags you down, don't be afraid to change course, even if it's only temporarily.

How much are you experiencing these emotions and feelings right now?

Date: [   ]

	NOT AT ALL	VERY SLIGHTLY	A LITTLE	MODERATELY	QUITE A BIT	EXTREMELY
ANGRY	☐ 5	☐ 4	☐ 3	☐ 2	☐ 1	☐ 0
ANXIOUS	☐ 5	☐ 4	☐ 3	☐ 2	☐ 1	☐ 0
CHEERFUL	☐ 0	☐ 1	☐ 2	☐ 3	☐ 4	☐ 5
HEALTHY	☐ 0	☐ 1	☐ 2	☐ 3	☐ 4	☐ 5
IN PAIN	☐ 5	☐ 4	☐ 3	☐ 2	☐ 1	☐ 0
LONELY	☐ 5	☐ 4	☐ 3	☐ 2	☐ 1	☐ 0
LOVED	☐ 0	☐ 1	☐ 2	☐ 3	☐ 4	☐ 5
MOTIVATED	☐ 0	☐ 1	☐ 2	☐ 3	☐ 4	☐ 5
TIRED	☐ 5	☐ 4	☐ 3	☐ 2	☐ 1	☐ 0
UNDERSTOOD	☐ 0	☐ 1	☐ 2	☐ 3	☐ 4	☐ 5

Add numbers beside checked boxes – Total A: [   ]

Multiply Total A x 2. This is your Well-being Score out of 100: [   ]

Plot Well-being Score on graph on page 280, then

...What happened?

Finally, if your score is...
0-42   Turn to Nudge 27C
43-67   Turn to Nudge 27B
68-100 Turn to Nudge 27A

Tidy space, tidy mind.

You can see how much of a big thing it's become to tidy your house when a Japanese organizing consultant is listed as one of the world's most influential people by *Time* magazine, as Marie

Kondo was. She's the author of the charming bestseller *The Life-Changing Magic of Tidying Up*, with a philosophy that boils down to three simple rules.

First, when you tidy, instead of looking for things to throw out, identify what you want to keep and only do this if the belongings "spark joy" (*tokimeku* in Japanese).

Second? Instead of tidying one room at a time, tackle your whole home in one go. Don't worry, though, Marie Kondo reassures us that once we've tidied properly, it will be a long time before we need to do so again.

Her third recommendation is to tidy by category, not by room. For example, gather all your books wherever they are, then keep just those which spark joy.

Not quite ready to give your home the full Kondo treatment? Perhaps her philosophy will at least inspire you to use your current good level of well-being to make a start. An orderly space could help maintain your elevated spirits.

What category of your belongings might need tidying?
E.g. Clothes, books, food

....

How would it feel to have it tidier?

....

When could you get down to this?

....

....

Don't spend hours on housework.

Just three and a half minutes.

On a day like this you might not be very excited about the thought of tidying up at home or work.

However, maybe a reminder that bringing order to your environment can often play a part in boosting mood and well-being could inspire you.

Perhaps you never seem to find time to address your domestic cleaning responsibilities? If so, why not think about committing to a three-and-a-half-minute session?

Yes, three-and-a-half minutes. That's all.

It's even possible, for example, to make a significant impact on a bathroom in just 210 seconds, particularly if you commit to doing the same thing for a few days in a row.

Make sure there are cleaning materials to hand (why not keep some in the bathroom itself, if you don't already do so?), then use a timer to give yourself no more than three-and-a-half minutes. If there's a timing app on your phone, use it, then clean like crazy when you push the Start button.

And when time's up, stop.

What will benefit from the three-and-a-half-minute treatment?

....

When can you schedule three-and-a-half minutes?

....

How do you think it will feel to do this?

....

....

Feeling down?
Tidy up.

However you currently feel, I'm sure you'll know that feeling of calm and order as you walk into a hotel room immediately after checking in.

Never mind what it looks like 24 hours later—it's that tidiness and simplicity as you first enter I'm thinking of.

Of course, in the same way that order can feel good, disorder can feel bad. When you feel low, though, the very idea of tidying up can be anathema, so you may grit your teeth and struggle on surrounded by ever-increasing chaos.

Please don't. I'm certain you'll benefit from taking the smallest steps to give yourself a more ordered living space.

Start small with just one drawer, but tackle it properly, ideally by removing everything and giving the interior a good wipe with a damp cloth. Then do your best to organize the drawer's contents as you replace them, but only put things back you really want to keep.

And rather than leaving yourself with a dilemma about whether or not to get rid of stuff, temporarily assemble your "discards" in a box elsewhere in the house, emptying it only after a week or so. This way you'll be less tempted to hang onto things simply because you're not sure whether you really want to keep them.

Do you have a messy drawer that's crying out to be tidied?

....

When could you set aside 15 minutes to tackle it?

....

(Later.) How did that feel?

....

....

28

Although most people go through spells when they feel they've little say in how they feel, perhaps working your way through the book is beginning to make you see you actually have more control than you thought?

How much are you experiencing these emotions and feelings right now?

Date: [ ]

	NOT AT ALL	VERY SLIGHTLY	A LITTLE	MODERATELY	QUITE A BIT	EXTREMELY
ANGRY	5	4	3	2	1	0
ANXIOUS	5	4	3	2	1	0
CHEERFUL	0	1	2	3	4	5
HEALTHY	0	1	2	3	4	5
IN PAIN	5	4	3	2	1	0
LONELY	5	4	3	2	1	0
LOVED	0	1	2	3	4	5
MOTIVATED	0	1	2	3	4	5
TIRED	5	4	3	2	1	0
UNDERSTOOD	0	1	2	3	4	5

Add numbers beside checked boxes – Total A: [ ]

Multiply Total A x 2. This is your Well-being Score out of 100: [ ]

Plot Well-being Score on graph on page 280, then

...What happened?

Finally, if your score is...
0-42   Turn to Nudge 28B
43-67   Turn to Nudge 28A
68-100 Turn to Nudge 28C

Albert Einstein, woolly thinker.

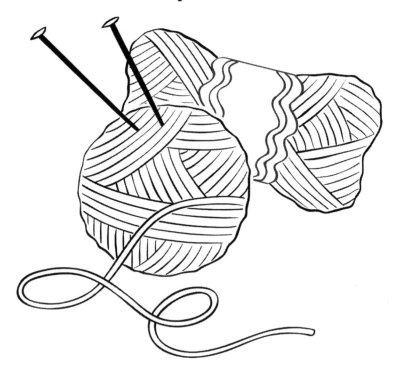

Did you know that Albert Einstein was a big fan of knitting, apparently?

Me neither.

Actually I would have had him down as more of a macramé man, myself.

All joking aside, it's said that Einstein employed knitting to clear his mind, and there's a good deal of evidence to suggest he was wise to do so.

When psychologist Mihaly Csikszentmihalyi identified a state of consciousness he called "flow", he explained that our brains can only process so much information at any one time.

When we create something, our existence outside of this activity becomes temporarily suspended.

Making things can be a helpful way to reduce stress and increase happiness, which makes it a rewarding activity to add to your schedule.

So ask yourself what you've crafted or made in the past that occupied your whole mind. Maybe it will work again.

What making or crafting activities have you enjoyed in the past?

....

Is there anything stopping you from doing so again right now?

....

What will you make, and when will you make it?

....

....

Make things better.

What were you good at making when you were a child? For me it was little books (See? I started early) and I well remember the satisfaction and full focus of crafting something. Perhaps it was the same for you?

Psychologists call this state of total preoccupation and absorption "flow", and one advantage of it is that when your mind is in this mindset you're almost certainly not going to think about being depressed or anxious. It's as if your absolute concentration leaves no room for unwanted thoughts.

Knowing all this, should you happen to be struggling through one of life's wobbly patches it's worth remembering that making something may provide at least temporary relief.

Perhaps you could bake a cake. Or draw a picture. What about fixing something that's broken? That's a kind of making. Even folding a sheet of paper into an airplane counts as handicraft. It could help to remember things you enjoyed building or baking as a kid. Why not enjoy doing so again?

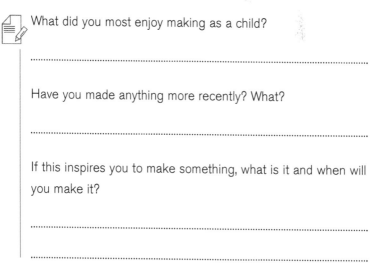

What did you most enjoy making as a child?

....

Have you made anything more recently? What?

....

If this inspires you to make something, what is it and when will you make it?

....

....

Craft yourself a better mood.

If you were a world-class athlete you could be forgiven for imagining your training days were over. Not likely, however.

In fact it's said that the average elite athlete trains for around 23 hours a week, which only goes to show how hard you have to work to keep yourself at the top once you reach it.

Actually, what holds true for sport may also do so for well-being, although I believe we sometimes think about this in a corrective way.

It's the approach taken by many healthcare professionals—something's wrong so we'd better fix it.

Surely a better way to view it is in a preventive way, the approach healthcare could take but unfortunately rarely does—nothing's wrong so let's make sure it stays that way. After all, isn't an ounce of prevention worth a pound of cure?

You're probably riding high in the well-being stakes at the moment, so let's keep it that way.

One equivalent to an elite athlete's training schedule is to recognize the powerful positive impact that crafting and making things can have on us.

Neuroscientist Kelly Lambert says engaging in arts and crafts can help keep depression at bay, and doing so bathes your brain in feel-good chemicals, creating a kind of "mental vitamin".

And it's always good to take your vitamins.

What might you enjoy making in the next few days?

....

Do you need to prepare for this?
E.g. Get materials or ingredients

....

What do you think it will feel like to make something?

....

....

29

Tomorrow's your final day with the book, and while you're not quite at the end yet, why not plan to mark the end of the thirty days with a bang? Approach today with gusto. Look for all sorts of ways to lift your spirits.

How much are you experiencing these emotions and feelings right now?

Date: [   ]

	NOT AT ALL	VERY SLIGHTLY	A LITTLE	MODERATELY	QUITE A BIT	EXTREMELY
ANGRY	5	4	3	2	1	0
ANXIOUS	5	4	3	2	1	0
CHEERFUL	0	1	2	3	4	5
HEALTHY	0	1	2	3	4	5
IN PAIN	5	4	3	2	1	0
LONELY	5	4	3	2	1	0
LOVED	0	1	2	3	4	5
MOTIVATED	0	1	2	3	4	5
TIRED	5	4	3	2	1	0
UNDERSTOOD	0	1	2	3	4	5

Add numbers beside checked boxes – Total A: [   ]

Multiply Total A x 2. This is your Well-being Score out of 100: [   ]

Plot Well-being Score on graph on page 280, then

...What happened?

Finally, if your score is...
0-42   Turn to Nudge 29C
43-67   Turn to Nudge 29B
68-100   Turn to Nudge 29A

Pay attention now.

I'm sure most children are taught at an early age that you should treat others as you'd like to be treated yourself. It's known as the Golden Rule, appearing prominently in almost every major religion.

Although I really don't think you can argue with the logic of this simple philosophy, it didn't stop George Bernard Shaw taking a rather contradictory view.

"Do not do unto others as you would that they should do

unto you," he argued, "Their tastes may not be the same." I think he had a point. And in fact, a variation of the Golden Rule called the Platinum Rule suggests we should "treat others as they want to be treated." Easy to say, but not easy to do. For a start it means understanding how others want to be treated. What do they need? What works for them? There's only one way to know this, and that's to ask them, then really, truly listen (hard) when they tell you.

Treating someone as they want to be treated may not necessarily mean the action will be reciprocated. It may, but it also might not. Don't let this stop you, though, because caring for another human being in a genuine, selfless, and loving way can feel good in and of itself.

 Who in your life might benefit from being treated differently by you?

....

How could you initiate a conversation with them to learn more? You'll need to listen hard when you talk, so allow time and space.

....

....

(Later.) What do you now understand better about some ways in which they'd like to be treated?

....

....

NUDGE 29B

Knowing others care about you can boost your well-being, and if you're in need of a lift it's worth remembering that empathy is nearly always a two-way street. When you care about someone else, they're more likely to also care about you.

So my suggestion today is to look for chances to experience the act of understanding someone better. A helpful, if unexpected, way of doing this is to stop and think if you find yourself about to criticize someone. If they seem rude to you, or they're behaving in a way that's unacceptable, try to get to the bottom of why they might be doing so.

In the words of the old expression, it can help to imagine you were walking a mile in their shoes. What might their life be like? What could have led to them acting as they did?

When we think of others with compassion and understanding, it helps us become more compassionate and understanding towards ourselves.

Finally, as a closing thought, I enjoyed an alternative version of the "walk a mile" principle that I came across recently: "Before you criticize someone, you should walk a mile in their shoes. That way, if they don't like it, you're a mile away and you have their shoes."

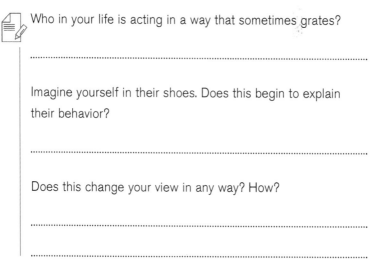

Who in your life is acting in a way that sometimes grates?

....

Imagine yourself in their shoes. Does this begin to explain their behavior?

....

Does this change your view in any way? How?

....

....

Get curious.

Next time you're troubled by the thought that nobody likes you and nobody cares, it might help to know that scientists take the view that as human beings we've actually evolved to care for one another and to cooperate socially.

So even when your mind tells you otherwise, science suggests that others will indeed be thinking about you. The trouble is that when you're battling through one of life's tougher patches, it may seem as though you're looking at things through a darkly-tinted window. On a bad day when you feel as though nobody cares, this can seem very real. What to do therefore?

Although it might sometimes be tricky, an excellent way to receive understanding is to give it in the first place. Try this today by showing real and genuine curiosity in a conversation with a stranger. Perhaps it will be the person sitting beside you on the bus or your neighbor in the supermarket checkout line.

If you break the ice with a simple "The bus seems busy today," or "I hope you don't mind me saying this, but I love the color of your jacket," a short conversation may ensue. Not always, but it's more than possible, and when it does, be sure to ask follow-up questions. It shows you care, and you're likely to feel the other person also cares when this happens.

Where might you be today when you could encounter a stranger?

....

What could you say to them to break the ice? Be a little brave.

....

Who do you know who's great at asking questions? Could you model the way they behave?

....

....

30

30 days ago you began a journey. Is this your final destination? Probably not. As we've already seen, the road to happiness is a long and winding one. But that's not to say you shouldn't be proud of your progress. Although there may still be a way to go, you've made real progress getting this far.

How much are you experiencing these emotions and feelings right now?

Date: [   ]

	NOT AT ALL	VERY SLIGHTLY	A LITTLE	MODERATELY	QUITE A BIT	EXTREMELY
ANGRY	5	4	3	2	1	0
ANXIOUS	5	4	3	2	1	0
CHEERFUL	0	1	2	3	4	5
HEALTHY	0	1	2	3	4	5
IN PAIN	5	4	3	2	1	0
LONELY	5	4	3	2	1	0
LOVED	0	1	2	3	4	5
MOTIVATED	0	1	2	3	4	5
TIRED	5	4	3	2	1	0
UNDERSTOOD	0	1	2	3	4	5

Add numbers beside checked boxes – Total A: [   ]

Multiply Total A x 2. This is your Well-being Score out of 100: [   ]

Plot Well-being Score on graph on page 280, then

...What happened?

Finally, if your score is...
0-42   Turn to Nudge 30B
43-67   Turn to Nudge 30A
68-100   Turn to Nudge 30C

Get scent back in time.

Have you ever been caught unawares and transported back in time by the unexpected whiff of a long-forgotten fragrance?

Perhaps a stranger passes in the street, wearing perfume or cologne that connects you to a time, place, or person in the past.

It may not happen every day, but when it does it can be a very powerful experience. Dr. Mason Turner, Chief of Psychiatry at Kaiser Permanente in San Francisco, says: "Scents bring up memories the way no other senses can. They can be very powerful in jogging fond memories."

Why not take advantage of this phenomenon whenever you need a lift?

Simply uncap a bottle of something sweet-smelling that takes you back to happy times.

There's nothing wrong in keeping a little bottle of scent for a rainy day.

What's more, some smells are mood-lifting in their own right, including basil, bergamot, clary sage, geranium, jasmine, neroli, petitgrain, rose, sandalwood and ylang-ylang (I love geranium and ylang-ylang).

Could this be a good day to introduce a little light aromatherapy into your life? I think it may be.

What scents do you associate with past happy times?

....

Could you introduce these, or one at least, into your environment?

....

What do you need to do to make this happen?

....

....

Exercise them all.

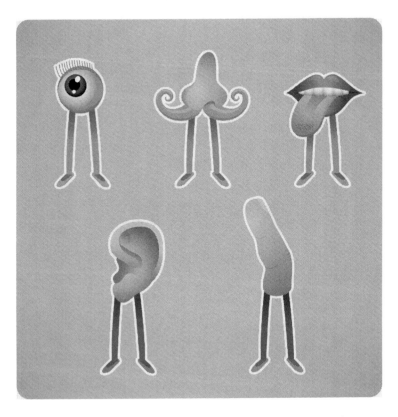

It's common to label the work psychotherapists and coun-selors do as talk therapy, and it seems perfectly logical that when you're dealing with low mood or depression it can help to talk things through with someone sympathetic and understanding.

In fact simply listening to another person being reassuring can be, well, reassuring. Sometimes it's easy to lose sight of the fact that what we hear can help, and this applies to sounds just as much as it does to talk.

But why stop at just one sense when you have five at your beck and call?

Today's a day to be fully aware of all your senses, seeking every opportunity to savor tastes, smells, sounds, sights, and touches that have the potential to help you feel good. Take time to enjoy your food, even if it's a simple dish. Be aware of the scents surrounding you, introducing soothing new aromas if you can. Listen to music that reminds you of good times, or simply tune in to the small sounds that make up your environment. Look around you, paying full attention to everything in your field of view. Touch different surfaces with your eyes closed, and enjoy the way they make you feel.

Soothe your senses in the coming day.

How can you introduce new calming tastes, smells, sounds, sights and touches into your day?

....

When will you do this?

....

How do you imagine you will respond?

....

....

Feel better.

On a good day like today, your senses will probably work overtime. Colors may seem brighter, and you'll probably be more sensitive to smells, both good and bad.

Make the most of it, and don't lose sight of the fact that all your senses are heightened. Stimulating any of them can help keep your spirits high.

Take touch, for example. Some people see hugs and physical touches from others as extremely important, so if this the case for you, feel free to make today a Day of Hugs.

However, even if you're not a touchy-feely person socially, you might find it's helpful to reach out and touch a variety of surfaces today.

Run your hands over fabrics and stroke your own hair—or the fur of a cat or dog. Walk barefoot. Gently massage your forehead. Wash your hands mindfully, especially if there's scented soap involved.

Since touch is the first sense to develop in babies, perhaps it's a good day to return to your roots?

What tactile sensations work well for you?

....

How do they make you feel?

....

How can you build some of this into the coming 24 hours?

....

....

31

It's a great day to look back at how far you've come.

Well done—and thank you—for working through the thirty days of *Nudge Your Way to Happiness*.

If you started the process by completing the online questionnaire mentioned on the book's first page, it would be enormously helpful if you could complete another one (actually with the same questions) so we can explore whether your time with the book has made any measurable difference to your mood.

Please only do this if you filled in the first questionnaire. Thanks for helping.

You'll find the second test online at:

moodnudges.com/endbook

Welcome to Day 31. Huh? The front cover of this book positioned itself as the "30 Day Workbook for a Happier You", and you've now made your way through 30 days.

So what's with this "Day 31" then?

Quite simply it's an opportunity for you to look back at the past four weeks in order to reflect on what you've learned, at least at what I *hope* you've learned.

John Dewey was an early 20th century celebrated psychologist, philosopher and educational reformer, who famously said: "We do not learn from experience... we learn from reflecting on experience".

I think that's true, even though we often carry out this kind of reflection in an unconscious way. For once, though, let's be a bit more methodical about the process.

Researchers at Harvard Business School said that reflection as part of learning can be expressed in three stages: synthesize, abstract, and articulate. If, like me, you struggle to grasp these rather obscure labels, let me do my best to put them in plain words for both of us:

1. Begin by combining a number of separate ideas into a coherent whole (*synthesize*).

2. Then look for patterns and themes (*abstract*).

3. Finally, express the ideas you've identified (*articulate*).

You may have discovered, as others who have worked through early drafts of the book have, that you've become more self-aware in the past 30 days.

Perhaps you've never experienced an introspective exercise quite like this one before? It would be a crime to allow this self-knowledge to slip through your fingers, so let's see if we can adopt the Harvard Business School approach to reflect on something rather closer to home.

Your own emotional health...

1. What things did you notice? Here are a few prompts, but please feel free to make a note of anything you experienced as a result of working with the book.

What did it feel like to rate your well-being every day? Did your experience of this change in any way across the 30 days?

....

....

....

....

How did it feel to get a nudge every time you recorded your score? How helpful was this? Were some nudges better for you than others? Did they encourage you to take action? Did you notice your behavior changing in any way?

....

....

....

What was it like to see your graph build up over the 30 days?

....

....

....

....

Was plotting your graph something you looked forward to?

....

....

....

....

At what time of day did you sit down with the book? How did that work for you?

....

....

....

....

Did you share your progress with anyone else during the 30 days? If so, who did you share it with and how did that feel? How much did you share? If you didn't share, what stopped you? How do you feel about that?

....

....

....

....

2. Now let's look at patterns and themes which may have emerged:

What do you see when you look at your graph? Was there an overall trend across the 30 days? If so, was it upwards, downwards, or level?

....

....

How did your scores tend to vary day to day? Did they change a lot, or a little? Did you notice patterns?

....

....

Did your score regularly rise or fall on a particular day of the week, for example, or did it do so when you found yourself in some kind of repeating situation?

....

....

What did you observe from the nudges? Can you draw any conclusions from the way they made you feel?

....

....

....

Did you tend to react to certain kinds of nudges in certain ways? Which nudges, if any, made you feel good?

....

....

....

Were some types of nudges less helpful? Was there an overall pattern to this?

....

....

....

Might your well-being scores have been influenced by things that were happening in your day-to-day life? Can you see any patterns in the kinds of things that made you feel good, and the other kinds of things that made you feel less good?

....

....

....

....

3. Finally let's see if you can draw some conclusions, and articulate your learning. What are the three main pieces of insight you've had from working with the book?

....

....

....

What are two things you might be able to do more of as a result of using the book?

....

....

....

Are there two things it might help to do less of, with your new-found self-awareness?

....

....

....

How do you feel overall about your experience with the book? What worked? What didn't?

....

....

....

Is there something you might change because of your new insight? What is it and how do you think you could make this happen?

....

....

....

....

Are You a Happiness Saboteur?

What are you doing to undermine your own emotional well-being? Find out how self-destructive you are—in just ten questions. Turn the page to start the test.

Are You a Happiness Saboteur?

Read the ten statements then decide how much each is like you, or not. Check the appropriate box and please be honest—there are no right or wrong answers. When you've finished, turn the page to see how to score yourself.

---

1. **When I'm having a hard time it's sensible not to make plans**

   Very much like me ☐

   Mostly like me ☐

   Somewhat like me ☐

   Not much like me ☐

   Not like me at all ☐

2. **On walks I get easily distracted by things around me**

   Very much like me ☐

   Mostly like me ☐

   Somewhat like me ☐

   Not much like me ☐

   Not like me at all ☐

---

3. **It seems best for me to keep my own company when I feel low**

   Very much like me ☐

   Mostly like me ☐

   Somewhat like me ☐

   Not much like me ☐

   Not like me at all ☐

4. **I like to know I'm living a life that has meaning and purpose**

   Very much like me ☐

   Mostly like me ☐

   Somewhat like me ☐

   Not much like me ☐

   Not like me at all ☐

5. I wish I was someone other than the person I've become

Very much like me ☐

Mostly like me ☐

Somewhat like me ☐

Not much like me ☐

Not like me at all ☐

6. It's hard to do things for others when it's me who needs the help

Very much like me ☐

Mostly like me ☐

Somewhat like me ☐

Not much like me ☐

Not like me at all ☐

7. It's really up to me to give myself a lift when I'm having a bad time

Very much like me ☐

Mostly like me ☐

Somewhat like me ☐

Not much like me ☐

Not like me at all ☐

8. I wait for things to blow over when I feel low

Very much like me ☐

Mostly like me ☐

Somewhat like me ☐

Not much like me ☐

Not like me at all ☐

9. I don't know it all— I think I still have a lot to learn

Very much like me ☐

Mostly like me ☐

Somewhat like me ☐

Not much like me ☐

Not like me at all ☐

10. I go to bed and get up at roughly the same times each day

Very much like me ☐

Mostly like me ☐

Somewhat like me ☐

Not much like me ☐

Not like me at all ☐

Are You a Happiness Saboteur? *(See previous page)*

How to score the test

A. For questions 2, 4, 7, 9 and 10 assign the following points:
0 = Very much like me
1 = Mostly like me
2 = Somewhat like me
3 = Not much like me
4 = Not like me at all

B. For questions 1, 3, 5, 6 and 8 assign the following points:
4 = Very much like me
3 = Mostly like me
2 = Somewhat like me
1 = Not much like me
0 = Not like me at all

Add the scores to get a total between 0 and 40. The higher your score, the more you're doing to limit your happiness potential.

What your score means

35 or more:

Possibly without realizing it you're actually doing a lot to sabotage your own happiness.

Your fairly high score suggests that you may struggle more than most when it comes to recovering from setbacks.

You probably don't have a kind of instinct for the things that will help, so might find yourself engaging in self-defeating behaviors that leave you feeling worse rather than better.

All's not lost, however, because mood management is a set of skills that anybody can pick up at just about any stage of life.

It's never too late to learn.

Now you've seen how the test was scored, why not start the process by looking back at the answers you got a high score for?

Doing this might provide you with some important clues about techniques that could work better than those you tend to automatically employ.

26-34:

While you're not the world's biggest happiness saboteur, you might not always behave in ways that are in your own best interests. But this doesn't mean you get everything wrong.

Indeed you do have a good grasp of some of the techniques that lead to happiness, and help to pick you back up again when things go wrong, which they're bound to do from time to time.

It's worth remembering that happiness habits are like a muscle that can be built up through regular exercise.

It can also help to be open to new ideas. Treat these like experiments, trying them out with an open mind, then hanging on to those that work, discarding those that don't.

15-25:

In terms of sabotaging your own happiness you're thankfully not doing too much of it.

In fact you're better than many at understanding how to maintain a healthy and positive mood, and you're also probably good at knowing how to bounce back from life's trials and tribulations.

You may also know how important it is to maintain any skill, which is exactly what managing your mood is. A skill.

The keenest knife only stays that way through regular sharpening. So by all means make full use of what you already know, but don't be afraid to take advantage of chances to learn new techniques, putting them into practice whenever possible.

14 or less:

Congratulations, you tend to be the architect of your own happiness rather than wielding a wrecking ball.

You have an excellent instinct for doing the kinds of things that can lead to happiness.

Living your life in this way makes it more likely that you won't find yourself suffering from a low mood, but if you do (and to a certain extent it's bound to happen on occasions) you'll almost certainly know how to get back on track again.

However, even though you're something of an expert at the happiness game, please don't get complacent. Even elite athletes have to keep on training, so always aim to be conscious of your thoughts and what you're doing, and never turn your back on an opportunity to pick up and develop new skills.

Many thanks to Action for Happiness, whose "10 Keys to Happier Living" inspired this questionnaire. See: actionforhappiness.org/10-keys-to-happier-living

Putting *Nudge Your Way* to the Test

Way before I even started writing this book I was adamant that I had to find out if its system would actually work. After all, you'll hopefully spend 30 days making your way through it. The very least I could do was test its approach.

So in what I think you'll agree is fairly unusual for a book, I set out to run a trial. If I gave a few people a prototype of the kind of book I planned to write, might they literally find themselves being nudged towards happiness? Or would it all fall flat on its face?

With the generous cooperation and support of 35 volunteers, I tested a draft seven-day version of *Nudge Your Way to Happiness* during the summer of 2015. Just as I've invited you to do (see the very first page of this book) the people who road-tested the prototype completed a short online questionnaire before and after working their way through it. As a matter of fact the questionnaire was a test called the PHQ-9 (the nine-question Patient Health Questionnaire) often used by health professionals to see if someone is suffering from depression, and if they are, to what extent.

Since the PHQ-9 is a tried and tested measure of mood, I was interested in seeing if the participants' scores might change between Day 1 and Day 7 of the experiment.

A helpful professor of neuropsychology at the University of California, San Francisco School of Medicine suggested that I should use the PHQ-9 in the first place, but he also cautioned me not to expect a great deal of change in seven days. He explained that although the questionnaire is considered reliable, it tends to be relatively insensitive to small changes in mood, which is all he expected me to find.

I was understandably pleased therefore to discover that, on average, those who used the book for a week did indeed get lower depression scores on the PHQ-9 than they'd shown seven days before.

Of course I'd also collected the participants' well-being scores as measured by the book. These rose quite appreciably across the seven days, suggesting that people had become happier.

PHQ-9 scores (maximum = 27)
Lower scores mean less depressed

Out of **23** people...

15 scores went down

5 scores went up

and **3** remained the same

by an average of 5.0 points

but by an average of only 1.8 points

Now of course this wasn't a clinical trial. We have no way of knowing whether people were just getting better of their own accord or if their moods had perhaps improved simply because they felt good about taking part in the research.

In fact these are just the same kind of issues that arise when new medications are researched, and it's why randomized controlled trials are used by scientists.

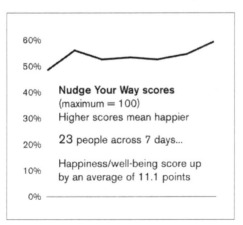

60%
50%
40% **Nudge Your Way scores**
(maximum = 100)
30% Higher scores mean happier
20% 23 people across 7 days...
10% Happiness/well-being score up
by an average of 11.1 points
0%

Maybe that sort of rigorous study lies ahead for this book, but for now it seems good to know that it certainly appears to be working along the right lines.

As more people use the full book, we'll gather more data about its validity. I'm pretty sure there have been few (if any) other self-help books which contain a built-in measure of their own effectiveness. I'm happy we're breaking new ground.

Acknowledgements

The nudges for Day 24 of the book are all about gratitude. Being genuinely thankful for the good things in your life—and expressing your gratitude to the people who contribute to it—is a brilliant way to help yourself feel good. With this in mind it does indeed feel amazing to be able to say thank you to the very many who have both contributed to this book and to the work that has led up to it.

Special thanks of course to Alexandra Carmichael, Samantha Carmichael Reda, and Megan Carmichael Reda for making me so warmly welcome immediately I arrived in California, patiently filling in countless questionnaires for me, helping to make stuff, and generally being all-round stars.

A loving thank you to my Mum, Joan Cousins, who encouraged me to take the leap to the U.S.A., and also taught me just about everything I know about empathy.

I dearly wish my Dad, Mike Cousins, could still have been around to see this book produced. I think he'd have been proud, because it was he who lit the publishing flame in me at a very early age (mine, not his).

Huge thanks to my brother Geoff Cousins and his wife Gill. They've both been a massive support through the years, and frankly without Geoff's help this book would have been a shadow of its present self, and might well never have appeared, to be honest.

Thanks to Seth Godin and Charles Duhigg for their kind endorsements of the book and for being generally inspirational, the same of which must be said of Chris Guillebeau.

Next I'd like to thank some of the hugely knowledgeable people who taught me so much about the mind and also helped me look after my own. Dr. Glenn Wilson started the process over twenty years ago, forgiving my beginner's knowledge of psychology while teaching me a huge amount. When we talked, Maria Arakie never failed to magic up delicious food for us all to share. There's clearly a refreshment thing going on here because the other psychologist who helped in spades was David Moxon, who essentially took me through a full psychology degree course on Friday nights in the Fox and Hounds. In California, Dr. Paul Insel has provided wise psychological counsel, strangely enough often over lunch. Annie Wilson was a lifesaver when my own mind wobbled, and has also been a source of great wisdom while I developed my mood tracking tools. Big gratitude also to Dr. Roy Baumeister, Dr. Martin Seligman, John Tierney, and Dr. David Watson for visionary work on whose foundations I've built. Grateful mentions, too, for Bob George, Katie Hart, Dr. Belinda Lennox, Dr. Sandy Lillie, Dr. Liz Miller, and Dr. Stuart Whomsley. Also a big thank you to Dr. Scott Mackin at UCSF School of Medicine, and Philip Insel at San Francisco VA Medical Center, for helping me understand how I should validate *Nudge Your Way*'s well-being test.

Over the years I've been fortunate enough to meet many members of the media who have "got" my work. Nicholas Roe wrote a thoughtful piece about Moodscope for *The Times* of London which got the whole thing started. Libby Purves invited me to be a live guest on BBC Radio 4's *Midweek* programme, attracting so much interest from new Moodscope subscribers that the web server practically melted. Sophie Morris wrote a long, intelligent piece for *The Independent*. Thank you, too, to other good friends in media circles who have all been interested and supportive, including Harry Beer, Andy Burrows, Lynn

Cardy, Nicholas Hellen, Sarah O'Grady, Sanne Rooseboom, Mike Scialom, and Paul Stainton.

Mark Williamson and Action for Happiness occupy a particularly special place in my heart and mind. I've learned enormously from Mark and AfH's ground-breaking work in understanding how happiness works.

UnLtd in London generously supported Moodscope with grants, but in some ways even better than the funding was getting to know people like Mohammad Al-Ubaydli, Neil Basil, Belinda Bell, Jo Hill, Dan Lehner, Emma Morris, Zoë Peden, and Cliff Prior.

I moved on from Moodscope in 2013 but still owe a debt of gratitude to my co-founders Caroline Ashcroft and Adrian Hosford who supported Moodscope's development and have kept it running following my departure. Thanks also to developer-extraordinaire Stephen Coote.

I consider myself deeply fortunate to have come across the Quantified Self (QS) in 2010, when Gary Wolf, a contributing editor at Wired and the co-founder of QS (also now a good friend) wrote about Moodscope in *The New York Times*. QS has been a kind of family for me and my connections with it flourished, introducing me to two awesome American friends. Josh Manley and I chat on the phone once a week, and I meet Raj(iv) Mehta once a month to walk and talk. There are many other QS friends but a special mention for Kate Farnady, Steven Jonas, Gustaf Kranck, Adriana Lukas, Ernesto Ramirez, Greg Schwartz and Steve Souza. Seth Roberts, too, was a great friend and visionary who left us way too soon.

Friends who've stoically tolerated me talking (and talking) about my "mood stuff" include Tony and Mira Rocca, who've been enormous supporters all the way and many times generous hosts. Christine Morgan has taken a close interest in all I've done over the years and been a willing guinea pig for more than a few new ideas. Thank you Christine. Thank you, too, Claire Insel in California for being an enthusiastic and insightful trial-ist of the full version of *Nudge Your Way to Happiness*.

Back in the U.K. Velma Wilson is a dear friend. Vince and Filomena Terranova run the splendid Buttercross tearoom in Peterborough, where I first put my cards (the Moodscope ones) on the table for others to see. The Buttercross was also where I met Jonny Groves, now in Israel, who became my first Moodscope "buddy" before I'd even considered that someone watching over you might be a thing. I met Jane Pope at an evening class in psychology. She's a great friend who's helped shape my work more than she knows.

A big thanks to other loyal and supportive friends, including Georgia Artus, Pippa Artus, Toby Ashcroft, Louis Ashcroft, Rodger Ashcroft, Simon Brett, Mike Burdzinski, Jill Carpenter, Annamarie Castrilli and David Carmichael, Ali Chadwick, Sadie De'Roux, Hamish Elvidge, Jeff Fanning, Emma Freud and Richard Curtis, Nicky Freud, Stephen Fry and Jo Crocker, Richard and Yve Hawkins-Adams, Matthew and Ainsley Johnstone, Peter and Beverley Learoyd, Jo and Paul Mallinson, Bob and Joy Mower, Mary Nolan, Dave and Di Oatley, Linda Paulson, Ruth Peasgood, Suzie Roberts, Juan Roman, Will Rowe, Paul Strayer, Sid Tomkins (thanks for invaluable design help with the book), Jayne Widdowson-Allen, and Susan Williams.

Over the years I've had a delightful relationship with many thousands of Moodscope members and Moodnudges readers, and am indebted to them for their support, enthusiasm and suggestions. A number of Moodnudges readers generously helped trial the *Nudge Your Way to Happiness* idea early in the book's development. Sincere thanks to Kathleen Alberter, Sally Baines, Marianne Barreiro, Louise B, Miranda Beere, Jo Blackshaw, Claire Brayne, Sarah Campbell, Wendy Carlton, Andrew J Chandler, Ryan C, Elisabeth Cook, Shelley Foster, Helen Fraser, Danielle Fryday, Hannah Gration, Sally Groom, Julie Hamilton, Julie Hemingway, Joanna Hudson, Jane K, Caron Kirkham, Darla LaRoche, Mary Lawrence, Naomi Long Srikrotriam, Eve Robinson, Martin Rowlands, Dee Ruddock, Janis Rushe, Pat Tonkin, Dorine Urrunaga, Jackie Ward and Claire White.

Last but not least, many thanks to Olivia Serene Lee and Tammy Kettler for their most excellent professional support.

Even with such a long list, of course, I'm sure to have left someone out, and I'm sorry about that if it's you.

Perhaps my next book should be *Nudge Your Way to a Better Memory*.

The main text font used in *Nudge Your Way to Happiness* is Classical Garamond, a typeface based on an original created by Claude Garamont in the sixteenth century. Garamont, widely recognized as one of the leading type designers of all time, was apprenticed to the King of France's official printer, Geoffroy Tory, an engraver maybe best known for introducing accents on letters in French. Sadly Tory's daughter Agnes died from unknown causes at the age of nine. Regrettably it was common for children to die young in those times, but apparently Troy took Agnes's death particularly hard, and it's said that he spent much of his later life suffering from depression as a result. It's thought-provoking, however, that the loss of his young daughter reportedly inspired great creativity in Troy's later works. Perhaps even the darkest of clouds can sometimes have silver linings?

About the Author

Jon Cousins is a creative entrepreneur who has learned how to successfully manage the depression he's had for most of his life.

After starting and running a successful London ad agency, he spent a year exploring the world, returning to the U.K. to launch a series of innovative online businesses in children's learning and online dating—using a psychometric matching technique developed with psychologist Dr. Glenn Wilson.

Despite outward success, Jon has battled with depression since his 20s, finally seeking help when he was 50. A psychiatrist asked him to keep a record of his own emotional health. In order to do so he devised a card-game mood test which provided daily scores that could be tracked on a graph.

The results confirmed the diagnosis leading the psychiatrist to encourage Jon to offer his tracking system to others, which he did via Moodscope.com, an online tool supporting thousands, and rated #1 in a U.K. Department of Health poll. Some Moodscope users credit the service with saving their life.

His work and methods have been examined and reviewed by, among others, *The New York Times*, the BBC and *The Times* of London. In 2013 Jon relocated to California after receiving U.S. government "extraordinary ability" status to further his mental health work.

www.nudgeyourway.com

@nudgeyourway

Author photograph: Jason Han

DAYS 1-15

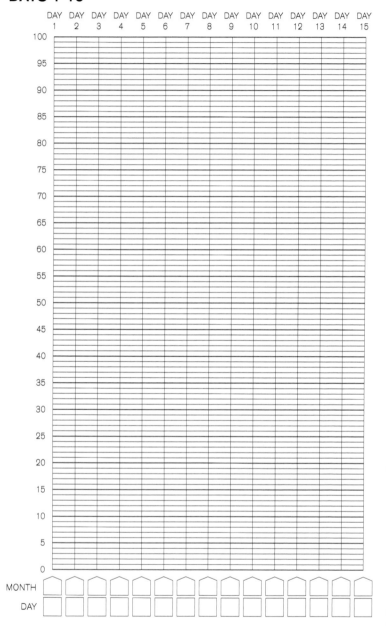

DAYS 16-30

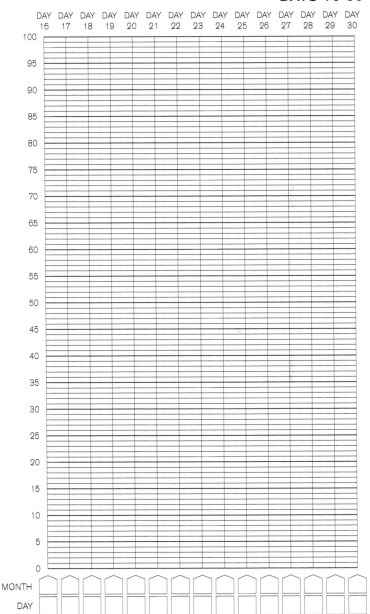

How to Get More Nudges

If you've enjoyed *Nudge Your Way to Happiness* why not keep the nudges coming by email? Sign up on the Moodnudges website to receive free four-times-a-week messages direct from Jon Cousins prompting you—just like the nudges in this book—to take small actions today, designed to help you feel a little better tomorrow.

At Moodnudges.com you can also interact with thousands of other readers by leaving your thoughts and reflections:

www.moodnudges.com

The WellBee Cards

The well-being test used in *Nudge Your Way to Happiness* is also available in the form of an ingenious "card game" called WellBee, consisting of hexagonal playing cards that allow you to choose the degree to which you feel each of the same ten feelings and emotions monitored in *Nudge Your Way to Happiness*. When you've done this, it's easy to calculate your overall score. WellBee would be useful if you wanted to keep track of your well-being without using this book, say. Also, therapists and counselors use WellBee as a way of checking in with their patients and clients. You can find out more about WellBee here:

www.wellb.ee

Made in the USA
San Bernardino, CA
07 June 2016